Sky Above Kharkiv

SERHIY ZHADAN

Sky Above
Kharkiv

DISPATCHES FROM THE
UKRAINIAN FRONT

Translated from the Ukrainian by
Reilly Costigan-Humes and
Isaac Stackhouse Wheeler

A MARGELLOS
WORLD REPUBLIC OF LETTERS BOOK

Yale UNIVERSITY PRESS | NEW HAVEN & LONDON

This book consists of material originally published in Ukrainian on Facebook. A version of this book was published in German as *Himmel über Charkiw: Nachrichten vom Überleben im Krieg* in Germany by Suhrkamp Verlag in 2022.

Yale University Press books may be purchased in quantity for educational, business, or promotional use. For information, please e-mail sales.press@yale.edu (US office) or sales@yaleup.co.uk (UK office).

Set in Source Serif type by Karen Stickler.
Printed in Canada.

Library of Congress Control Number: 2022948315

ISBN 978-0-300-27086-0 (hardcover : alk. paper)

A catalogue record for this book is available from the British Library.

This paper meets the requirements of ANSI/NISO Z39.48-1992 (Permanence of Paper).

10 9 8 7 6 5 4 3 2 1

Introduction

Writing contradicts death. The desire to capture feelings and meaning, circumscribe accounts, and relay story lines fundamentally clashes with the idea of ruin, destruction, and disappearance. We cling to the writing process as an illusory chance to pin down and preserve the outline of reality, flee the energy field of extinction, and try to trick oblivion. How justified is this illusory state? Well, it's at least a constant of sorts—most of us are inclined to cling to time, to the feeling of it, to its passage.

So how do you pin time down within the confines of your consciousness, within the confines of language? You can try writing. Even if what you've written won't become literature. Moreover, who is there today who can clearly define the boundaries of literature, its contours, its frontiers? What we attempt to get out, shout out, and put out there every day—is that literature? Is there some sort of line of demarcation between what we are willing to say and what we want to read?

On February 24, 2022, a full-scale war began in Ukraine. The regular army of the Russian Federation appeared on Ukrainian territory, the shelling of Ukrainian cities began, the destruction of our country began. We faced a choice—either hold out and survive or be annihilated. I never thought I would construct a sentence like that on my laptop. It's quite possible that on February 23, I would have found that kind of phrasing too pretentious, excessively emotional—perhaps even ideologically colored. But when you get a call and are told that your friend who received a vehicle from you the previous day has apparently been killed and can't be buried because his head is nowhere to be found, you realize that these words are the most precise and truthful for all us Ukrainians these days. We don't have much choice—withstand this war or be annihilated. That's the way it is. There aren't any other options or any other scenarios. Whether you are a writer, an IT specialist, a municipal worker, or jobless, if you take Ukraine's side, you become a potential enemy for the occupier, and you could potentially be annihilated. Even if you don't take a stance, you could still be annihilated. We have all been targets since late February; we have all come under fire, regardless of our views. This speaks to our vulnerability. But it does not mean we feel helpless or doomed.

A lot of residents have left Kharkiv, the city where I live, since Russia began its full-scale invasion. Probably hundreds of thousands. A lot of people have stayed, though. And many of those who have stayed made a conscious decision to do so, so they could defend the city and keep working. Some have gone off to the front lines. Others have stayed back to volunteer on the home front, helping servicemen and civilians. For me personally, it was and still is a great honor to know these people, to have the opportunity to stand alongside them under the springtime Kharkiv sky, to have the opportunity to say something about them, to write something about them, to snatch their voices, their shadows, their figures out of a great stream of time.

Why have my friends and I stayed? Because we have a lot of work to do. We had this work to do before February 2022, too, and it hasn't gone anywhere. We knew that when the occupiers came we wouldn't be able to hide out in basements, that we would have work to do instead. Second, and probably more important, we love this city too much to abandon it when it's going through tough times. So we decided to stay put in the neighborhoods we're used to, where we've always felt calm and confident.

War contends with language. During times of war, you constantly catch yourself thinking that you lack words. It's like you've had your breath taken away, the wind knocked out of you, so words get lost, spill all over, and seem misplaced. This is a very strange feeling, strange and unpleasant, because it contains too much anger and too much powerlessness. You can't stop this evil, and you can't find the right words to articulate what you've seen. Reality winds up overpowering language. Reality needs new words, new intonations; it demands that all the most important things and phenomena be renamed.

Over the years, I've gotten used to writing something on Facebook every day, and it has turned into a job or sorts. A diary for everyone, I guess. It's mostly about what's going on. Well, and I've gotten used to posting all my new poems online. There's this direct response from readers, so you can fix, edit, or rewrite something right away. That isn't an option with poems in black ink. The spontaneity, openness, and uncensored quality of it is what makes readers reacting instantly on the internet so appealing. Sometimes, naturally, this stresses me out or bothers me, but all in all, what could be better than a sense of connection crafted by language, by the written word?

About a week after the full-scale Russian invasion, in early March, I noticed that I was unable to read: it was hard to focus on anything besides the nightmarish news that kept coming in. You notice that when you pick up texts they simply fall apart, spill all over, like sand running through your fingers; you can't grasp on to them, you can't stop their flow. Something similar happened with writing, too. You can't write, because this process doesn't feel all that appropriate. War sharply changes ways of seeing, changes feelings. Above all, it immediately changes the weight of a great many things, things that seemed necessary and obvious just a day ago. And it turns out that after the first residential areas are bombed, the very notion of a metaphor seems suspect. Just like turning current events into literature, molding reality into literature, searching for images and similes, using blood and gore as literary material seems ethically dubious and completely inappropriate.

I'm fully aware that this isn't anything new—art locking up in the face of death, observing, spellbound, the world splitting and being transfigured, losing its former traits and its former meaning forever, as something significant, something implacable and irreparable unfolds underneath its outer crust. You can't pick the words to feel or guess what exactly is unfolding. You can merely give names to everything you see, to what your vision captures, to what your vision hurriedly and chaotically focuses on, and do so out loud. I doubt you can call that literature. I'd say it doesn't have to be clearly defined, though. Maybe later, when this war ends, we can return to the terms used in literary criticism. That's probably how things will play out. For now, none of this is about literature—it's about reality.

Naturally, these posts were not written as a book. That just came down to the need to remember the faces, names, attitudes, hopes, and disappointments I encountered these past few months. My greatest fear was that this temporal and spatial content, this bulk of joy and misfortune, faith and pain would simply evaporate in the past, like a chunk of March snow in running water. So I wanted to capture and preserve all of this, keep it written down, articulated, as something that receives another chance—a chance to be heard, a chance to be understood. Later, when my friends first suggested I make a book out of these entries, I thought that might be the best manifestation of love and reverence for those mentioned in them. Or for those who weren't mentioned yet whose shadow was near, one way or another.

There are a lot of names here which probably would not have appeared in any other, more conventional work; however, in these diary entries, they feel natural: the people of Kharkiv who became witnesses of history, witnesses who weren't always the most talkative, yet were almost always honest and responsible. They are all a testament to the misfortune that has been brought upon us, the misfortune we're counteracting. They are the true heroes of this book: epic, comic, lyric, but first and foremost, truly human.

I don't know how things will stand on the front lines when this book is published. In Ukraine, we naturally all believe our country will win this cruel war. Moreover, we're working toward our victory, giving up our lives for it. Yet we are well aware that this victory probably will not come easily, and it is unlikely it will come quickly. We are ready for that, though. We are willing to defend our country; we are willing to stand up to aggressors and war criminals. Because we have this feeling of what is our space, our soil, and our sky overhead. This book is about that, too—this feeling of a sky that has your back, that illuminates you, that marks the outer limits of your presence in the world.

One more thing—this story isn't over. This diary of a city that we folks from Kharkiv love so much is still being written. Chronologically speaking, my title is limited to the first four months of Ukrainians' armed resistance. And as I wrap up this short note, I'm aware that soon it will be six months since the Russians launched their invasion. To a great extent, that doesn't change much. The war continues; it keeps exhausting our country and taking our citizens' lives. Yet our resistance continues, too, keeping the absolute evil the occupiers have brought with them at bay. Nobody will strip us of the right to call the country where we were born ours. And nobody will strip us of the right to speak our language. We don't always have sufficient resources to speak to this evil and be treated as equals, yet our language has turned out to be much stronger than any attempt to compel us to remain silent, to forgo calling a spade a spade, or to forgo pronouncing the names we use to identify each other. We are trying to stand up to death; we are trying to stand up to absolute silence. We reserve the right to speak the truth: the truth of this war, the truth of this time, the truth of the voices that evaporated into the sky and made the air more translucent—and more potent.

Serhiy Zhadan
August 1, 2022

A Note on the Text

The following texts were published on Facebook between February 24 and June 24, 2022, during the first four months of the full-scale Russian invasion of Ukraine. Emoticons have been retained where they appear in the Ukrainian texts. Ellipsis points in square brackets indicate extraneous material that has been deleted, such as bank information, contact information, embedded hyperlinks, or captions for images that do not appear in this translation.

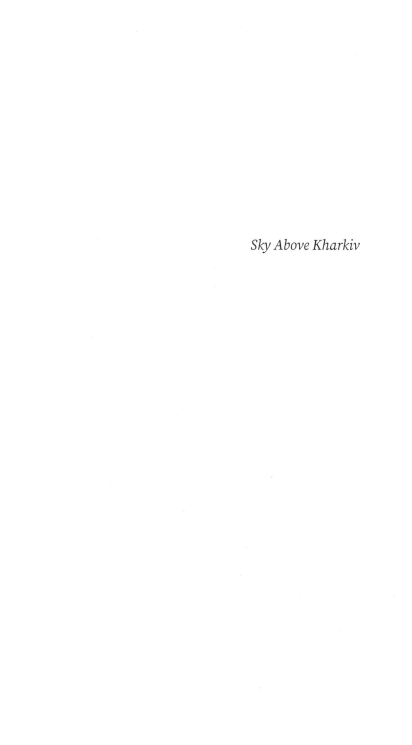

Sky Above Kharkiv

February 24, 3:50 p.m.

Video Transcript
Serhiy Zhadan with his band, Zhadan and the Dogs, standing by the Kharkiv Region sign

Hi, everyone. We were on the road all day, and now we're heading home because this is where our homes are, this is where our families are, and this is our place.

All our concerts will come later, after we win. For now, we'd like to encourage everyone to stay where they belong and do their work, to support the Armed Forces of Ukraine, and to assist our fellow citizens, who need our help today.

Remember one thing, my friends: this is a war of annihilation. We cannot afford to lose—we must win.

So let's stick together.

Glory to Ukraine!

February 26, 4:45 p.m.

We drove all around the city—went to Bavaria, Os-
nova, near the airport, the city center, North Saltivka,
regular Saltivka :), the Kharkiv Tractor Plant, all the way
to Proletarska in the east (that's as far as we were al-
lowed to go), Moskalivka, and Kholodna Hora. People
are somewhat alarmed, but there's no sense of panic.
There are a lot of police officers on the streets detain-
ing people who might be up to something. We stopped
a few, too, asked them to show us their phones and not
to take videos of our servicemen. They understood our
point and agreed. :) Yesterday we stopped by the airport:
our guys responded within ninety (!) seconds, knocked
us down into the snow, and then got our autographs. :)
The professionalism of Ukrainian servicemen is truly
something to see. They're all motivated, eager to rip our
enemies to shreds. I saw a line of men outside a con-
scription office—they all want to take up arms. I stood
by a tent in the square nearby for all of ten minutes and
within those ten (!) minutes, several cars full of supplies
for the army pulled up and three men asked where they
could sign up for the Territorial Defense Forces. Then
we drove over to the edge of the city heading out toward
Lyptsy. Our guys over there feel very confident. They
mentioned that the enemy keeps sending column after
column that they have to fire at— and that's exactly what
they've been doing. :) We talked for a little, and then they
got word on their walkie-talkie that another column was
approaching from the outer ring road. We were asked to

leave, naturally. As soon as we drove away, the enemy really started walloping the city. The pictures of the playground in North Saltivka floating around the internet are from that offensive. Our servicemen are monitoring everything on the road up to Rohan. They're advising people not to go any farther. It was quiet in Kholodna Hora. An hour ago they started pounding us from the east. I couldn't tell you precisely where it was were coming from. Kulinichi started selling bread again. There are bread lines. There are lines everywhere, actually. The lines are calm, though; there's no panic or desperation in the air. We got some coffee at a little convenience store in Babai. As the clerk was giving us our change (he didn't know who we were), he said, "Glory to the heroes" in parting.

February 27, 9:49 a.m.

Good morning, everyone. We've been in touch with our volunteer units. They're really pounding the enemy in the city. Now I'd like to thank everyone who has supported our volunteer units this whole time, for the past eight years. These units are truly battle-ready. And for those who haven't supported them—well the way I see it, you're being killed by the Russians whether you like it or not. I imagine you don't. Kharkiv is fighting; you can hear the constant rumbling all around the city. Death to the Russian occupiers.

February 27, 7:26 p.m.

We spoke with the volunteer units that pushed the rest of the Russian column back to School 134, the one on Shevchenko Street. The school went up in flames. Along with the occupiers. It's a shame about the school. Can't really say the same about the occupiers. Fifteen dead, burnt-out equipment, four POWs—that's what they've got. Some of our guys were wounded, but they're all alive, thank God. Kharkiv is greeting the liberators with flowers. :)

February 28, 8:34 a.m.

You can hear all kinds of booming in Kharkiv. A lot of people are outside, though, standing in lines outside stores and pharmacies. There are a lot of servicemen checking up, monitoring things. Don't go outside without your IDs, my friends. Better yet, don't go outside unless you have to. We talked to our guys—they're a little tired after yesterday. We're holding the city. Ukrainian flags are fluttering above it.

February 28, 2:07 p.m.

We were driving around the city. Right before the shelling, actually. People are getting organized, helping each other out. There are food lines. And a lot of servicemen and police officers. They're eager and angry, expecting guests. We were on the outskirts of town. They're building checkpoints over there. Local guys are standing by with their hunting rifles. The Russians simply can't imagine what's in store for them here. We brought our boys two carloads of equipment. Businesspeople have been giving our volunteer battalions everything they have in their warehouses. They don't mince words about the occupiers. Grad rocket launchers are pounding Kharkiv, civilians are dying. The Russians aren't an army. They're a horde.

February 28, 3:04 p.m.

Let's talk about the school that got burned down yesterday, my friends. We got the scoop from our guys who stormed it. The Russians knew we were coming. They'd stocked up on provisions and even had time to set up machine guns. They did some serious prep work. It didn't help them, but still. What am I getting at? There may be saboteurs in the city. The police and military have been checking everyone very thoroughly. They checked us the other day, too, when we were going to pick up a generator. We reached a checkpoint: they stopped and detained us, took us down to the precinct, ran our information through their system, apologized—and then took pictures with us. Point is, be aware of your surroundings. Don't get in our servicemen's way. The Armed Forces of

Ukraine and the police are working hard, and they're doing a stellar job. Everything will be all right, everything will be Ukraine. :)

March 1, 7:36 a.m.

Kharkiv. They fired rockets right into the middle of the city, hitting civilians. The Russians aren't an army. They're criminals.

Residents of Kharkiv, please take care of yourselves. If you can, help those in need: food, medicine, transportation. Let's stick together. They can destroy our apartment buildings, but they can't destroy our contempt for them. And our hatred.

March 1, 4:30 p.m.

My friends, parliamentary deputies Mykola Blahovestov and Natalya Nakhnina from Vysokyi, who are trying to help their community, have asked me to share the following message. Go ahead and share it, too, as someone you know may be able to help.

The Vysokyi Community in the Kharkiv Region is in dire need of supplies, medication, diapers, and children's food. Our volunteers, deputies, and activists delivered grains, flour, meat, and cheese products, but unfortunately, it wasn't enough for the local population.

We're requesting assistance from those who can provide foodstuffs, financial support, children's food, and
diapers.

[. . .]

Glory to Ukraine.

March 2, 7:31 a.m.

Some businesspeople I know delivered several carloads of bread to the city. We've been helping out. We
unloaded one carload at Karazin University's dorms, and
people from the buildings nearby started lining up. The
rest of the cars will deliver bread all around the city. Basically, everyone who is able to collect aid for the civilian
population is doing so. Then the bombardment started.
The city center got hit hard. Right before that, I saw a column of foreign students, about a hundred of them, who
were trying to escape from the city. They were carrying
a flag—the flag of India, I think. We're holding Kharkiv.

March 2, 10:00 a.m.

I stopped by to take a look at the university. Here I am
standing in front of the busts of three Nobel laureates
from Kharkiv. They're a source of pride for Kharkiv. Just
like Karazin University itself, the oldest university east
of the Dnipro River. Now here it stands, windows shat-

tered. An army of Russians has been targeting Kharkiv's schools. Foreign students cannot escape from Kharkiv, a city of universities. The Russians are barbarians. They've come here to destroy our history, our culture, and our education, because all those things are alien and hostile to them. We have to protect all that, restore it, keep developing it. I say that as someone with an honorary doctorate from Kharkiv Karazin University.

Monuments at Karazin University (*left to right*): Nobel laureate Ilya Ilyich Mechnikov, 1845–1916; Nobel laureate Lev Davidovich Landau, 1908–1968; Nobel laureate Simon Smith Kuznets, 1901–1985.

March 2, 12:31 p.m.

Reminds me of the Second World War. I'm referring to the occupiers' ideology and moral imperative, first and foremost. They've come here to liberate us from us. They don't even have a compelling narrative for those with weak stomachs. They simply want to destroy us, just in case, just because.

I recorded several audiobooks at the Palace of Labor. That's where Zhadan and the Dogs have our studio. The Russians are barbarians. A war crimes tribunal awaits Russia. There's no other way.

March 3, 10:28 a.m.

Kharkiv is receiving aid from all over the country. This is truly very important—not just protecting the city, but protecting every single resident of Kharkiv. This is a place where we will always live and work. Friends, your support is incredible. You can really feel it, especially when Russian rockets are flying overhead. The Russians are barbarians. Kharkiv is holding on.

March 3, 12:57 p.m.

This came from Lviv in a box of medicine today. :)
Thanks, Marko and Liza!

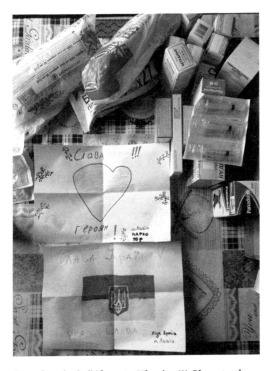

(*Top drawing*): "Glory to Ukraine!!! Glory to the
heroes! Lviv, Marko, 10 years old"; (*bottom drawing*): "Glory to Ukraine! Glory to the heroes! Liza,
8 years old, Lviv."

March 3, 4:50 p.m.

Share this, my friends!!!!!

The Department of Surgery at the Kharkiv Regional Clinical Hospital needs the following:

surgical kits for their operating rooms

kits for primary surgical treatment, a trepanation kit, bipolar coagulation, and suture material.

Contact person: Vitaliy [. . .]

Thanks to everyone willing to help!

March 5, 7:25 a.m.

Good morning, everyone. Greetings from the Kharkiv highway. :)

The sign reads, "Russian Warship, Go Fuck Yourself!!!"

March 6, 5:44 p.m.

Today, the sky above Kharkiv was high and trans-lucent, and the clouds were kind of vivaciously vola-tile. Heavy piles of snow fall from the roofs. It's quiet in the city itself, so people look around when they hear the snow fall. It's springtime in the city. It's wartime in the city. It's empty in the city center. There are more people once you get a little farther out. It's pretty lively outside the city limits. That may be because it was rela-tively quiet this afternoon. There are a bunch of our ser-vicemen here and a lot of guys from the Territorial De-fense Forces. It's a fortified city, basically. A very pretty, sunny, springtime city. Can't wait to rebuild it once we get rid of all this filth that has come here from the east and chuck it back across the border into oblivion. This place will continue to be the city of poets and universi-ties, you'll see. The Ukrainian flag is still fluttering above the city.

March 6, 7:51 p.m.

All right, let's talk about the context of Russian chau-vinism, with all its markers, stereotypes, and rigid stances. How much more limited can culture be than language? Take the language of a regular police officer (from now on, in Ukraine they'll be known as police offi-cers, not pigs) from Kharkiv, for instance. He's a Russian speaker, of course. But now he's digging through debris and pulling out Russian-speaking old ladies who voted for pro-Russian parties and who are being killed by air strikes launched by the president of a country that inherited "great Russian culture." In the context of history, this police officer is much mightier and more convincing than the whole imperial tradition with its Golden and Silver ages. He rescues people. The imperial culture kills them. Yes, that's right—the culture itself, and the whole fake, moribund context behind it that we're all used to putting up with because—well, because it's a "grand narrative." In actuality, it's a grand narrative that always justifies violence and disdain for others. That's really what it is.

In this war, culture has suffered a devastating defeat once again. This time, it's the "culture of Dostoyevsky and Tolstoy." And you can't really partake in schadenfreude here. Because in reality, the defeat of culture is civilians getting incinerated by Grad rockets. And servicemen, too, by the way. Clearly, it's hard to make any predictions during week two of World War III, but it's clear that—no matter how much longer our sublime and reckless world exists, no matter what subsequent configurations European civilization may take on (yes, the very same humanistic heiress of Athens and Alexandria that has tried to swallow the annexation of Crimea and Russian tanks in the Donbas for the past eight years)— Tolstoy and Dostoyevsky have suffered a devastating defeat. Just like the Russian ballet, the Russian avant-garde (which, to a large extent, is actually Ukrainian, not Russian), along with Russian hockey, and Russian soccer (well, that was going poorly even before the war). A people incapable of stopping itself before it bombed cities in a foreign country doesn't have the right to shift blame to a nominal adolf. Now it's your common burden. You're marked now, Fritz. That was a perfectly normal name before World War II, wasn't it? It's still a marker of sorts, though. That's how it'll go with your names now, too. So Dostoyevsky won't provide you with cover any longer. "Great Russian humanistic" culture is sinking, like the unwieldy *Titanic*. Sorry, I mean like the Russian warship.

P.S. The only consolation is that in sixty years, the next Tarantino will shoot a live-action movie about you. But in the movie, you'll be basterds. Inglourious ones.

March 7, 10:31 a.m.

A missile damaged the legendary Slovo Building, home of the great Ukrainian writers of the Executed Renaissance. This is perfectly natural for the Russians, as they've always destroyed our culture. They won't pull it off this time, though. The Russians are barbarians. And we'll rebuild the Slovo Building.

March 7, 9:44 p.m.

There's something else I'd like to talk about—choices. During a war, they emerge sharply, unexpectedly, and often unavoidably. Then from there, you make a decision—take some steps, muster the resolve, or shy away from things.

These days, it is the individuals I encounter who surprise and inspire me the most. Patrol officers and women volunteers, priests and drivers, special forces operators and villagers carrying hunting rifles. Beyond this, a deep, clear outline takes shape, the outline of a people that has finally recognized its own strength, the strength of its rage as well as the strength of its unity. Not an electorate divided among politicians, but a society politicians have—finally—started speaking to openly and honestly. It's crucial to acknowledge the trust and respect we have for each other at this particular moment so we can hold on to it after we win.

[. . .]

March 8, 1:33 p.m.

Today, the sky above Kharkiv is shrouded in large, anxious clouds. The sun pokes through occasionally, reminding us that it's springtime. It's gloomy when the sun is gone. Yet it's quiet. Soldiers say that's exactly what's got them worried. There hasn't been any bombardment, so people have poured into the streets. They're standing in line for humanitarian aid, and outside stores. Tough guys sit next to kiosks in their neighborhoods (we just drove around, like, half the city) and brashly munch on sunflower seeds. Reminds me of George Shevelov's accounts of Kharkiv during World War II. Nowadays, Shevelov sounds even more relevant. Just outside the city I saw a heart-wrenching picture: two dogs who had clearly been left behind by their owners were lying in the middle of the road because it was warmer there. Cars cautiously drove around them. Overall, everyone has become more conscious of others, more aware. The Ukrainian flag flutters above the city. We're holding Kharkiv. We just delivered a carload of medicine, stuff for children, and food, as well as several special orders (also medicine). And we're going to keep working. Thank you all for your help. If anyone else wants to chip in, here's Oleh Abramychev's card: [. . .]

March 8, 1:48 p.m.

Don't forget one thing, my friends. History isn't just being rewritten right now. It's being rewritten in Ukrainian.

March 9, 6:52 p.m.

For us Ukrainians, as soon as something big goes down, Taras Shevchenko quotes start popping up. That's how it was during all of our revolutions, and that's how it is today. The thing is, I can't picture the Russians reciting Pushkin as they go into battle, or taking to the barricades with quotes from Mikhail Saltykov-Shchedrin. Come to think of it, I can't really picture them taking to the barricades. :)

It's a good thing we have Taras Shevchenko. Happy birthday, Poet of the People!

March 10, 9:27 a.m.

Now you realize how important the past eight years were to us: years of real change. How much we've changed over the past eight years. The army, society, and the government itself. I realize that we Ukrainians love to grumble, but still . . . If the Russians had launched a full-scale war back in 2014, there probably wouldn't have been any unity or resistance. The Russians simply don't understand what has been going on here for the past eight years. That's where all their nonsense about denazification comes from. So what has been going on? We've been developing, while they've been decaying. And that's how things will keep going. :)

We packed a van with all sorts of useful stuff, and now we're on our way to Kharkiv. We're delivering medicine and groceries to several families. I wish you all the best.

[. . .]

March 10, 2:13 p.m.

Winter has returned to Kharkiv. In the morning, there was a dusting of dry, stinging snow, but in the afternoon, there's been a full-on blizzard out here, which makes the city seem so big and cold. A lot of trucks and minibuses are careening all over the city, delivering humanitarian aid. People are carrying bags of groceries that they've just received down the streets. We suddenly noticed that there was nobody on Pushkinska Street. Turns out that an air-raid warning was sounded. Residents of this city have learned to get off the streets quickly. Some people do keep going about their business, though. Overall, the city has organized itself quickly. Patrol officers are racing all around, and municipal employees are still collecting garbage. From underneath deep, fresh snow an outline of the city has emerged: a city we know and love, a city where we plan on living in the future. The Ukrainian flag flutters above that city.

March 11, 10:20 a.m.

The empty March streets of Kharkiv and the cold metal of tram tracks. The city has changed drastically over the past two weeks. You can feel the strength pushing through the pain. Saving the lives of those who live here is what matters most. The businesslike air and easygoing attitude innate to Kharkiv will return to the streets of the city one day, you can be sure of that.

Bottom line: this isn't a war between countries. This is a genocide of Ukrainians.

March 11, 7:05 p.m.

Yesterday we gave a fallen soldier's girlfriend a ride. She was coming back from the funeral. She was quiet, concerned about taking care of her grandma and grandpa, making sure they had their meds.

And a thought came to me: obviously all our assessments and emotions are, to a great extent, guided by the media landscape we choose (or which is imposed upon us). Go check out some popular Russian Telegram channel (since they don't have access to Facebook anymore), and you'll see they have a completely different reality, a completely different war: Ukraine is destroying its own cities, Ukraine is threatening the whole world, Ukraine is trapping its own citizens in besieged cities. They have a different reality; they view video footage of burnt-out Russian tanks as merely part of a counterpropaganda campaign.

Here's the deal, though—any media landscape, any propagandistic narrative is a collective thing. Curses and revenge are personal things, though. And the Russians will now have to live with this for a very, very long time, with our curses and our revenge. They're collective. And personal. Now they'll have to live with this.

[. . .]

March 11, 10:19 p.m.

And I'd like to make another point. I was rather skeptical of the current government. I was struck by one particular thing. The elections of 2019 brought a lot of young people to power—not my peers (I'm a far cry from being young) but a bunch of political youngsters who didn't belong to dozens of parties or hadn't worked for all kinds of shady cabinets of ministers. "But why do these young people," I thought, "act like old functionaries from the Kuchma era? Where did their childish urge to make a quick buck and flaunt it come from? Why aren't they trying to be different?" Thing is, I personally had the chance to do what I still consider rather constructive, useful things with a lot of them—everyone from ministers to mayors and governors. Nonetheless, I'd look toward the Parliament building and ask myself, "Why aren't you trying to be different?"

Now with the naked eye you can see them trying to be different. Advisers, speakers, ministers, negotiators, officers, mayors, and commanders—these forty-year-old boys and girls whose generation has been dealt the cruel lot of having to stand up for their country. And this applies no less (and possibly even more) to the millions of soldiers, volunteer fighters, and just regular people pitching in, people shedding the swampy legacy of the twentieth century, like mud falling off new, yet well-chosen combat boots. Young Ukrainian men and women —that's who this war of annihilation is being waged against. And then, in contrast, are the heads of Russia, Belarus, America, and Germany. The first two are old delusional geezers from the past century who look an awful lot like old Russian armored vehicles. Sure, they're technically armored vehicles, but they're old. And they're Russian, which, in itself, does little to recommend a vehicle. Then there are the latter two—they're cautious office clerks, retired capitulators who aren't brave enough to admit that they, too, are involved in what's going on.

Of course, I'm saying all of this without any sense of idealization (especially with regard to the political class) or, for that matter, nonchalance. Obviously, politics isn't a field whose harvest is capable of surprising us every year. Obviously, we all will continue to have a lot of questions, issues, and doubts. But still . . . it's Day 16 of the war. And this thought has come to me: history is a deft yet sometimes rather cruel potter. At times, it shapes our souls in ways we never could have guessed. Flames make it firm, naturally, but this invisible hand of history, of eternity—it alone is capable of doing incomprehensible things.

Let's keep believing in our country. Good night, everyone. Tomorrow, we'll wake up one day closer to our victory.

March 12, 9:24 a.m.

We bought equipment—almost 400,000 hryvnias' worth—for a volunteer unit we've been working with, so thanks a lot to everyone who's been helping out. This really is concrete, necessary aid that will be directed to the right people. Also, we loaded up tons of meds for two hospitals. Aid is coming from all over the country.

One more thing, my friends. My patience is significant, but I have my limits. All of us here are experts in anti-aircraft warfare and international politics, of course—otherwise, we wouldn't be here :)—but don't come here to spread panic. If you want to help out, then do it. If you don't, if you want to bad-mouth the military administration and write about how all is lost, go to someone else's page. During wartime, listening to the Ukrainian people cry about how traitors are behind it every time something goes wrong really gets to me. It's sickening.

As for asking, "Why isn't the government doing this?!" Having volunteers help out isn't a rebuke of the government, but rather proof that we're all in this together now. If you have a different view of things, I'd be glad to hear it. After we win. For now, I'm going to kick anyone spreading panic off my page.

All right, we're off to Kharkiv. Good morning, everyone.

March 12, 4:00 p.m.

It really was spring this morning in Kharkiv. You look at the sky, and your eyes tear up from the sunlight. Then there's a bang, and you automatically duck, notice the wet snow, the heavy, sticky black earth, and the gray asphalt. Municipal workers are out clearing the rubble and the snow. There are so many volunteers around town. They're quite visible—buses and trucks give them away. In the spring sun, residents of Kharkiv are out strolling, turning their faces toward the sun. Couples and young people walk or take trolleys from neighborhood to neighborhood. But this measured, almost lethargic cadence suddenly disappears when you see a little old lady hunched over, plodding home and pressing a fresh loaf of bread against her chest. At the same time, there are some oh-so-expensive cars flying by in the direction of Oleksiivka. And they're tailed by vehicles with servicemen inside them.

You get this strange feeling when a small, overtly hipsterish sedan stops outside an apartment building, and a fighter carrying a machine gun suddenly steps out. He has a bag of warm clothes, too. A girl comes outside. They talk for a while. He hands her the bag, lingers in the sun a moment, trying to warm himself, hops in his hipstermobile, and heads for the front line.

We drop off our meds at Hospital 4 and meet one of the doctors. "What's going on out there?" he asks. Clearly, he's so swamped with work that he can't keep up with the news. We tell him what we've seen and agree to bring more aid in a few days.

There aren't that many people out in the afternoon. Water drips from the eaves. The sun steadily glides away from the city. The shadows stretch. The evening encroaches. The anxiety mounts. The Ukrainian flag still flutters above our city.

March 12, 4:49 p.m.

I stopped home, took Oleksandr Rojtburd's artwork off the wall, and brought it to a safe place where it can wait out the bombardment. We have to pass on what's most important to our children: our culture—and our weapons. :)

March 12, 10:19 p.m.

Lately, the evenings in Sloboda Ukraine are as tense as the lungs of someone holding their breath. And the evening sky is special. Before I would have said it was Gogolesque. But no, it's not Gogolesque. It's Shevchenko-esque. Let's drop the Little Russian identity.

Dream happy dreams. Tomorrow we'll wake up one day closer to our victory.

March 13, 12:22 p.m.

A lot will be written and sung about this war. I suppose the language will be completely different: the language taking shape right here, right now, every day, across the whole country. As of now, it's filled with too much pain. There's certainly enough anger, though. And most important, there's enough faith and enough love.

Our guitar player Zheka Turchynov and I swung by a studio in Dnipro. Our friends from the band Vertep and us are trying to record something new.

March 14, 8:11 p.m.

Cold, March city. Artillery impacts have been shaking the air all day. We talk with friends we bump into around town. They all comment matter-of-factly, "That one's incoming, heading at us. That one's outgoing—we're hitting back."

Suddenly, I notice that the only people out and about are men: carrying groceries, volunteering, simply standing next to an apartment building and staring up at the sky. That's how we used to look out for snow. Now we look out for rockets.

The city is empty by a little after four. Everyone is getting ready for the night. I hope it will be a quiet one. Drivers race around, fast and focused. You can feel spring during the day. It gets chillier in the early evening.

Ukrainian flags flutter above the city.

March 15, 9:36 a.m.

It's sunny and empty this morning in Kharkiv. An air-raid warning just sounded. Spring feels sharp, heart wrenching.

March 15, 10:28 a.m.

Kharkiv, Sumska Street. One of the pictures shows what used to be a bookshop downtown. Does anyone still want to talk about Dostoyevsky?

March 15, 12:25 p.m.

These days, the sky above Kharkiv is vast and attentive. Like someone's eye.

March 15, 2:16 p.m.

These days, Kharkiv is akin to an ant colony that's been disturbed by someone's dirty boot: the ants' chaotic movements are actually indicative of well-coordinated, logical work. Everyone is doing what they should be doing. Everyone is where they belong. The ants are tending to their colony because they love it. :) Everything will be all right, everything will be Ukraine.

P.S. I just got done talking to our city council members and servicemen. They're all beaming with confidence. Ukrainian flags flutter above our city. :)

March 15, 8:12 p.m.

Let the sky above Kharkiv be quiet. Good night, dear brothers and sisters. Tomorrow, we'll wake up one day closer to our victory. I'm going to bed. I'm beat. :)

March 16, 7:43 a.m.

Last night was not a quiet one. After a patch of thick, compressed silence, blasts echoed and shook the air. It sounded like boxcars were being hitched together somewhere above us. People started driving as soon as curfew was over. The city is living its life. You can hear birds singing outside. Good morning, everyone.

March 16, 2:24 p.m.

Svyatoslav "Slava" Vakarchuk just paid us a visit. :) I asked him to bring a car and all kinds of useful things for our guys. Slava came through for us. Now our volunteer units have an armored vehicle as well as a ton of walkie-talkies and thermal imagers. That's just what they need—they're clearing the enemy out of the outskirts. Slava, buddy, thanks on behalf of Ukrainian Kharkiv. :)

We spoke to the mayor and the department heads. The city is living and working. Municipal workers are in close contact with servicemen. Everything is running like a well-oiled machine. The city is fighting.

We went down to the metro and spoke to Kharkivites. A lot of them have lost their homes. There's no sign of despair, though, just anger and a willingness to help.

We went to a hospital. Our medical professionals are simply fantastic—when an enemy sabotage and reconnaissance group broke through about an hour ago, they grabbed their assault rifles and encircled them. Once they took the Russians out, they returned to their operating rooms and got back to aiding our forces. I'll be sure to write a separate piece about the hospital.

To put it simply, I feel fortunate to live in this city. The residents of Kharkiv have shown so much courage, so much strength, and so much humanity over the past few days. I've never seen anything like it anywhere. Everything will be all right, everything will be Ukraine. Ukrainian flags flutter above the city.

P.S. There's a newborn in one of these photographs. This is Bohdanchyk. He was born during the war. His mom went into labor down in the metro, and then she returned to the metro after she had him. This here is our future. We're all taking a stand for Bohdanchyk.

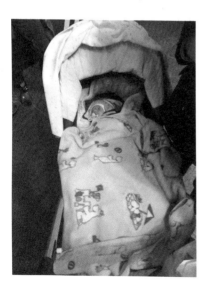

March 16, 3:00 p.m.

Friends, misfortune has struck one of our volunteers. I'd appreciate if you could help or just share this post.

Shared from Vasyl Riabko:

March 16, 12:55 p.m.

Today, as we were evacuating people from Saltivka, my friend, the driver of our bus and a volunteer, Anton Khrustalyov, was killed. I was next to him, but I survived. I wasn't even injured. This happened as the result of a peaceful neighborhood being bombarded with Grad rockets.

This was a typical evacuation. I was closer to a building, so I was spared. I had only known Anton for two weeks, but he had become a true friend. He was a good person, a pacifist. He signed up all on his own because he wanted to help people. We evacuated more than three hundred people, brought them meds and groceries, and helped the Territorial Defense Forces. He spoke Russian, and he was a regular old guy who grew up by the Kharkiv Tractor Plant. If he doesn't make it to heaven, I don't know who's up there. Today, he was killed by the Russian world—by those Russian brutes who came to liberate us. We had a lot of bread in our car today. He was a peaceful person, a private citizen who didn't want to fight. He helped people. Burn in hell, bastards. You'll answer for all this.

P.S. He leaves behind a daughter. The card number for donations to his family is in the comments.

March 16, 4:23 p.m.

The residents of Kharkiv are singing "Chervona Ruta" in the metro. This is history. And there's no place for Russia in this part of history. I love you all.

March 16, 8:02 p.m.

The employees at our hospital are brilliant, just incredible. Realizing that the invasion was inevitable, they decided to stock up on several months' worth of supplies. And they refused to leave. Individual stories about our medical workers will come out after we win. :) One more thing, my friends—I'd just like to tell those who still don't know what's going on here that this is a people's war. Ukraine has never experienced this before, but here it is. The whole city is against the occupiers. How exactly the Russian warship plans to settle down in these parts is beyond me. :)

March 17, 8:51 a.m.

History repeats itself in strange ways, going in circles and marking new routes. And the symbolism of these days is especially bitter and deep: the city under siege, fighting off the horde, people hiding in the metro like it's a church, united by song, men and women standing tall because the city has their backs and the city has to be protected. Everything suddenly became so lucid and expressive. This can no longer be erased, it will remain.

It was quiet at night, but come morning you could hear the bombardment again. The day began, the city came to life, and everyone is doing their work. Good morning, everyone.

[. . .]

March 17, 9:02 p.m.

The children of Kharkiv are drawing peace as rockets fall around them. And they're having art shows. Our children will have peace and their own country. Good night, friends. Tomorrow, we'll wake up one day closer to our victory.

March 18, 9:45 a.m.

It's sunny and translucent in Kharkiv. There aren't many people out. One might think it's Sunday. Unfortunately, the shelling continues, with these constant booming sounds. We're holding the city. Everyone is where they belong. My volunteer friends get to work first thing in the morning, taking in humanitarian aid, making lists of addresses, and delivering supplies. Hundreds of people are volunteering. Everyone has been united by the same goal: to hold out and win.

Ukrainian flags flutter above the city.

March 18, 12:03 p.m.

My "literary mother" is Olha Ivanivna Riznychenko. It was on her typewriter that I typed my first manuscript (is it still a manuscript if you type it, though?), which eventually became a book called *Quotations*. During the thirty years Olha and I have known each other, we've lived through a couple of revolutions and buried several people who were very close to us. Now we're going through this war. Olha has been a volunteer since 2014. Nowadays, she is running a volunteer center in Kharkiv that has helped a lot of people in town. I love and respect her fiercely. :)

Thing is, all these days full of war are also full of stories of insane courage and humanity. So many fates, so many eyes, so many hearts. Rockets can't knock out all this love and faith. Everything will be all right, everything will be Ukraine.

March 18, 3:46 p.m.

Over the course of the past eight years, I've probably had dozens of events in Germany. And despite the fact that most Germans had a pretty reasonable view of what was going on in Ukraine, supported us, and sympathized with our cause, I witnessed a lot of different things. I remember a debate I had at the beginning of all this, in March 2014, with a former East German general. I remember some people in the audience reacting enthusiastically when the general made remarks such as "Russia is entitled to Crimea," "Ukraine is wrong to resist," etc. I remember German Trotskyites handing out pamphlets at a book forum in Leipzig and saying that Nazis had come to power in Kyiv. I remember President Steinmeier somewhat wearily asking me about the situation on the ground in Ukraine. In short, I remember a lot of things. So when *Der Spiegel* offered me a chance to write a report from Kharkiv, I didn't hold back. Of course, this isn't an accusation aimed at all Germans. It's a reminder. A reminder that when you feed a rat for a long time it can grow into a real monster. What should be done about this monster? That's a question that now affects everyone, not just municipal employees in North Saltivka.

March 19, 8:57 p.m.

Kharkiv is getting bombarded once again, but the city stands. Because it's our city. We don't have anywhere to go. This is our home. We will protect it. Good night, dear brothers and sisters. Tomorrow, we'll wake up one day closer to our victory.

March 20, 9:59 a.m.

It's sunny and chilly in Kharkiv. There are a lot of people out and about. Seems like they're strolling around town just so they don't have to sit at home. Actually, though, everyone has gone out to do something: go to the pharmacy, pick up groceries, take someone somewhere. The traffic lights aren't working, but drivers politely yield to pedestrians. Feels like spring is just about to start for real. In the morning, there's talk among the volunteers about a car that has been repaired, meds that have been delivered, hot water that has disappeared, and who will be taking humanitarian aid where. Everyone is talking on the phone: some are offering help, others are asking for it. The city is upbeat, yet a little chilly. Ukrainian flags flutter above the city.

March 20, 5:05 p.m.

Injured, yet unbreakable. I really love this city and the people who live here. We'll restore everything. We'll fix everything. And we'll put up a wall along our eastern border so we won't be able to hear a single voice coming from over there. Glory to Ukraine. :)

March 21, 9:11 a.m.

Spring has come to Kharkiv for real. The streets are hot and sunny. The birds are singing louder and louder—drowning out the sirens. :) The people on the streets give one another inquisitive looks, more hopeful than mistrustful. Overall, everyone has become more aware of others. Life goes on in the city center: folks are handing out humanitarian aid, neighbors are just hanging out and chatting. They don't pay any mind to the explosions you can hear on the outskirts of town. They're used to it by now. As you walk around the city and talk to friends, you catch yourself thinking that Kharkiv is now one big volunteer center, though it isn't always visible. It's a city with a big heart and incredible humanity. Ukrainian flags flutter above the city. :)

March 21, 11:07 a.m.

There are new sounds in the cityscape. When you walk down the street, broken glass crunches sharply under your feet. In the older sections of the city center, destroyed buildings are already being cleared, storefronts are being repaired, and municipal workers are taking care of business. We have a lot of work ahead of us. But it's good, honest work. It doesn't scare us. We'll restore everything. We'll rebuild everything.

March 21, 12:51 p.m.

I stopped by a volunteer center the other day. Some young, truly young people were working there, and one thing I noticed was how important and natural it was for them to speak Ukrainian. These days, that indicates that they're different—proves it, in fact. It's a marker of sorts for them, and it will always be with them. The Russians' bungling incompetence really comes down to the fact that they didn't even bother to learn anything about us. Therefore what they considered a weakness has, thus far, turned out to be an advantage and source of strength for us. So let's try to keep that up. :)

March 22, 1:41 p.m.

Kharkiv today. People have been cleaning up outside their buildings, sweeping up bricks and glass. We're used to our city being clean. :)

March 22, 7:28 p.m.

Kharkiv kids are singing the national anthem down in the metro. Four weeks of war.

Today, my poet friends, some actors, and I put on a concert for the people staying in the Kharkiv metro. I've honestly never heard such genuine applause. In the evening, right before curfew, people in Kharkiv try to make the best use of their time by walking their dogs or going out with their kids. There is an unexpectedly large number of cats on the streets. :)

Have a quiet evening, dear brothers and sisters. Tomorrow, we'll wake up one day closer to our victory.

March 23, 7:51 a.m.

For the first three weeks, I couldn't read anything except the news. Then I got my hands on a collection by Maik Yohansen, one of my favorite writers, and started rereading it. It's miraculous just how well the sounds and voices of Kharkiv in the 1920s resonate with what's going in the city today. Like a sturdy thread, Ukrainian poetry stitches up the body of history, holds everything together, doesn't let us forget a single thing.

Good morning, everyone. Greetings from Ukrainian Kharkiv. We all have a lot of work to do today.

March 23, 11:29 a.m.

There's something poignant about watching the street sweepers of Kharkiv these days. They clean up thoroughly, unhurriedly. There are still some snowbanks around, but it's hot out in the sun, and wearing winter clothes is uncomfortable now—spring is here.

Most passersby have plastic bags—they're carrying something from somewhere. I ran into an older couple. They recognized me, said "hello," and wished us victory in the war. :)

After the initial shock and shelling, the owners of the cute little restaurants and boutiques downtown have been repairing and reinforcing their damaged storefronts and tidying up inside. We went to the destroyed university athletic complex and dormitories. The Russians dropped three bombs on the athletic complex. In other words, it wasn't an accidental hit. They targeted it. And the complex itself and two dormitories have basically been destroyed. Luckily, nobody was injured.

There is a lot of foot traffic on Pushkinska Street and tons of cars downtown. The city is being cleaned up, put back together. :) Street cats hunt pigeons. :) Ukrainian flags flutter above the city. :)

March 23, 7:00 p.m.

Almost a month of war. The city, which initially experienced shock, has bounced back quickly, rallied, and put up stiff resistance, despite daily (mostly nightly, actually) shelling and constant casualties. These are miraculous stories of people who didn't cower in fear but rose to the defense of their city, their country, their future.

Seeing kids soaking up the spring and racing down the streets on their scooters is particularly sublime. We recently had another concert in one of the metro stations. People are a little weary, but they haven't lost their faith. Life goes on, people are thinking about the future.

Have a quiet evening, everyone. Tomorrow, we'll wake up one day closer to our victory.

March 24, 10:34 a.m.

There were loud explosions last night. The official report is that they were missiles fired from ships in the Black Sea Fleet. This morning, there was a lot of shattered glass on the sidewalks again. But there were a lot of street sweepers, too, as well as citizens using brooms to clean up outside their buildings. At this time of year, Kharkiv is very gentle: the snow has nearly vanished, the ground is drying out, it's still damp and empty, yet you can already anticipate the greenery. Dust whirls up and down the streets—we're a city out in the steppe, after all. :) Also, there's a lot of garbage from all the destroyed buildings. The municipal workers are out first thing in the morning, though.

I caught myself thinking that today was the first time in two weeks I'd spent money—actually stopped by a store and bought something. :) Before that, I was running back and forth between volunteer centers, so I didn't really need anything. :) Some stores are open—not all day, but still. Naturally, prices aren't what they were like prewar, but they're reasonable. No profiteering or anything like that. People are navigating these new conditions, looking for ATMs and places where they can buy water or pick up supplies. I'd like to say that life is returning to normal, although the correlation between rocket fire and normalcy is kind of weak.

I just saw this old guy. He was clearly calling his friends. "I'm outside. Bring me a chessboard." :)

The sirens just came on again. Ukrainian flags still flutter above the city.

March 24, 6:20 p.m.

I walked past an art studio. Somebody had patched up the busted windows with their paintings. So heart wrenching and melancholy. The city is defending itself.

I met up with some friends. They told me that a spy had been caught. She was walking around taking pictures and filming, and asking a bunch of questions. Most notably, she spoke Russian with "not our accent."

When you're out and about a lot, you wind up meeting friends. There I was, walking around town when I heard someone hollering. Turns out it was the Kharkiv Region's deputy governor. He's been riding around working, not wasting any time. He told me a little about how things stand. It's tough, but there's no need to panic.

My volunteer friends made a trip to Dnipro to pick up some supplies. They got their car washed while they were at it—they've been all over the place the past month; they even got caught in a Grad bombardment in Saltivka. The car had lost its original color. Now it's all clean and shiny, a car for aesthetes.

Have a quiet evening, dear brothers and sisters. Tomorrow, we'll wake up one day closer to our victory.

March 25, 10:23 a.m.

Kharkiv cats. Sad. Yet proud. There really are a lot of them around town. People have been feeding them. We just visited a woman who is taking care of seventeen cats—her neighbors left them. These are some miraculous stories of humanity and compassion.

March 25, 12:05 p.m.

In the morning, ringing silence pervades Kharkiv's neighborhoods. After the nighttime shelling, all you can hear in the air is our occasional outgoing fire.

I bumped into a couple of retirees. They were out looking for a pregnant cat they hadn't managed to feed the night before.

Two cheerful homeless guys were sitting outside a pharmacy. One of them was shooting a bright toy gun. The other was laughing. Guess that's how this time and place feel to them. There's smog in the city—smoke wafting from Gagarin Prospekt.

We delivered aid to neighborhoods all over the city. Some people were sitting at home; others were hiding in basements. Besides that, large groups of municipal workers were out collecting garbage. More little stores were open—people are establishing new lines of communication.

We headed outside the city to pick up a car that was just repaired. Some local mechanics have been repairing cars for our forces. For free, of course.

"So have any of the locals gone off to fight?" I ask.

You're kidding, right?" they say with a laugh. "There aren't any spots left in the Territorial Defense. It's all filled up. *Everyone* signed up."

Outside the city, spring is in full swing—people are sitting on benches and listening to the sounds of the city. Smoke hovers over the city. And Ukrainian flags flutter. :)

March 26, 9:36 p.m.

Our friend was killed. He was the commander of a unit we have been helping out for several years, not just the last month. Zhora was the kind of man who always led from the front. It was remarkable. And it elicited respect. Since February 24, I've mentioned several operations in which the Freikorps, the unit commanded by Zhora, took part. They were the ones who took the school on Shevchenko Street. They were the ones who caught those Moskals in the forest park. To a great extent, they were also the ones who cleared the occupiers out of Rohan, where Zhora perished. For the enemy, that may be a success—I don't know. For us, this is one more reason to fight for our land. The Freikorps has lost its commander, but it hasn't lost its motivation. And now it will take revenge. I don't envy the Russians posted outside of Kharkiv, especially knowing how yesterday's battles in Rohan went for them. Friends, remember Zhora—he's a true hero of this war. There will be a street named after him in Kharkiv one day, I'm sure. Thanks, buddy. It was an honor to stand next to you. Fly high.

March 27, 5:59 p.m.

Winter has returned abruptly. Wearing sneakers isn't all that comfortable. :)

Slava Vakarchuk called this morning and said that he'd brought a Starlink kit for the Freikorps. He asked me to find him a guitar, and we met up by our pal Taras.

Several cars stopped while Slava was singing. People took videos without getting out and then kept driving. One woman was crying while she was filming.

A bearded man who looked like an apostle was walking down Sumska Street, holding a cardboard sign against his chest that read, "Ukraine will win."

We paid the unit a visit and drank some tea to Zhora's memory. The boys are anxious, but they're also angry and amped up. In the afternoon, we had a concert in a bunker to support our Territorial Defense Forces. Several dozen people who are dear to me came—wasn't expecting that. Poets, musicians, actors—everyone was there, everyone was where they needed to be. It reminded me of the music festival in Eskhar (people who aren't from Kharkiv may not get the joke)—there was just as much shit on the table. :)

I met up with Yuriy Butusov. He told me a lot of interesting stuff about what's happening on the front lines. Can't share everything, sorry—but it's good news, trust me. :) There aren't many people out. First off, because it's cold, and second, because it's Sunday. In Kharkiv, people stay at home on Sunday—even the municipal workers are resting.

The city is calm and quiet. Heavy clouds blacken the sky. It's supposed to be sunny tomorrow, though. Ukrainian flags flutter above the city, the cold wind snatching at them ferociously. But that just makes them whip and blaze even more. Like birds. Or sails. :)

March 28, 1:48 p.m.

We've covered about half the city. When you're driving around, you suddenly realize just how big and varied it is.

In North Saltivka, garbage collectors scour the side of the road as smoke rises dramatically on the horizon. People catch the sun's warm rays and clear the rubble. Wrecked buildings are cold and damp inside. Scattered possessions are like dead guts. Winds roam down hallways and stairwells. Glass crunches underfoot. We delivered a washer to a hospital, took it straight out of an apartment that had been destroyed. I called the doctor.

"Come out and meet me," I said.

"How will I recognize you?" she asked.

"I'll be holding a washer," I said.

At one of the train stations we passed, there were some men pushing a switch engine. I'd never seen that before. :) They pushed it out of the way, then ran over and started giving us hugs—turns out they were book publishers from Kharkiv. :)

There was a dog sleeping outside the hospital. Purebred, had a collar. It had clearly been left behind. Now it lived with the doctors.

At Barabashovo Market, a wonderful woman gave us several boxes filled with slippers and underwear. We were asked to thank the vendors at Barabashovo on camera, which I'm more than happy to do. Their flair is incredible, just amazing.

We delivered some insulin to the hospital and other meds to people all over Oleksiivka. The springtime sky hangs high off toward Derhachi.

Moskalivka is quiet and dusty, yet cozy. Spring is here.

People are a little tired, yet they aren't intimidated. They live, love, and won't give up. And it goes without saying—Ukrainian flags flutter above the city. :)

March 28, 3:38 p.m.

We made it to the store before curfew and bought a chainsaw. This will come in handy for the boys getting ready to welcome the Russians to Ukraine. :)

Friends, you can't even imagine how strong the armored carapace being built around you is—and you're helping make that happen. But you can, though. You can see everything for yourselves. A completely different country, a strong, proud, and remarkably humane one, is being built. Well, how are you gonna get any building done without a chainsaw? :) So thanks for your help. We've already handed it over to our boys.

Have a quiet night, everyone. Tomorrow, we'll wake up one day closer to our victory.

March 29, 11:05 a.m.

We said our goodbyes to Zhora. The boys are composed and sanguine. Overall, it's hard to describe all of this with ordinary words, which by now have acquired a completely different significance. Faces illuminated by candles that burn so slimly, fighters saying goodbye to their commander, stepping straight from the church into battle. Weapons thumping against bulletproof vests. The priest held the funeral service while outgoing artillery fire shook the air—our forces were hard at work. It's striking just how well equipped our boys are—Zhora poured his heart into his job and left us with a very powerful unit. In the candlelit church, the fighters looked as though they were ancient icons. There is a strange, painful feeling of history taking place right here and now, and against this backdrop new Ukrainian forces, a new generation of Ukrainians, and a new country are taking shape. Take care, my friends. May you all be among the living today.

The inscription reads, "Glory to Ukraine! Glory to the heroes!"

March 29, 12:38 p.m.

Meanwhile, our insanely mobile team drove around, like, half the city again in our somewhat beat-up Hyundai: delivering and passing things on, picking people up and seeing them off. :) We helped evacuate an old-timer from a hospital—thanks to Nastia Hrynova for her help.

We bumped into some members of the local and regional governments and spoke about Mala Rohan—our forces really walloped the Russians there.

A police officer ran over while we were standing around talking.

"There was a man filming without permission here," he said.

I let him go, though. They chased after him and eventually caught him. :) Turns out he was an old friend of mine.

"He's on our side," I told the police officer. "Let him go."

He let him go, thought for a bit, and then asked, "And who are you? Are you from the security service?"

"I'm the alternative mayor around here," I said. "Give me a call if you need anything."

"Ah, I know who you are. I wanted to sign up for the security service, but I got rejected—I rub people the wrong way sometimes. So I decided to become a fire-fighter."

Now more and more stores are open in the city. Thrift stores are back in business, too. :) The prices in a butcher shop in the city are much lower than at the market outside town. :) There aren't any lines, except at the post office and the beer store. Squills bloom a burning blue in the city. Ukrainian flags flutter above the city.

March 29, 8:52 p.m.

My volunteer friends and I are sitting around getting all our plans squared away: delivering meds, passing along bulletproof vests, and prearranging humanitarian aid. Have to find it, drop it off, and divvy it up. Most solutions are quick and easy: everyone is conscious of others, supportive—even if they can't help someone, they know someone who can. Tomorrow is a new day: lots to do, new tasks, new objectives. This is our city. We love it, and we won't let anyone else have it. :)

Take care of each other, my friends, and believe in our country. Tomorrow, we'll wake up one day closer to our victory.

March 29, 9:29 p.m.

All right, my friends, we have a problem. A few days ago, somebody requested markers for the kids staying in the metro—but I don't remember who asked me and where—there's so much going on—so I don't know where to bring them! But I bought eight sets for you. Speak up, whoever asked for them. I'll give them to you tomorrow. Gotta keep drawing. Good night, everyone.

March 30, 1:11 p.m.

I've noticed that great Ukrainians cast long, expressive shadows here in the city. The philosopher Hryhorii Skovoroda worked here (to paraphrase Pavlo Tychyna's line "Skovoroda walked here"), right here, behind these cinder blocks; the writer Mykola Khvylovy lived here, in this building, next to where a shell just landed; Shevelov lived right here, and so did historian Dmytro Bahaliy. This is a major Ukrainian city that has always given the country so much, yet it has been otherized and singled out with such gusto by so many. "We all have relatives in Russia"—that's been a common refrain. :) Well, I've lived my whole life along the Ukrainian-Russian border—Russia was basically in my backyard—but I don't have any relatives in Russia. :) And thank God for that. :) All right, I don't want to start anything. We're holding Kharkiv. It's springtime in Kharkiv. Ukrainian flags flutter above the city.

March 30, 2:54 p.m.

Time for our regular segment "You Asked for It, We Did It." :) The markers have been delivered to the kids. As well as a mountain of art supplies. Because Ukrainian kids are creative and talented. They're camping out down in the metro, drawing, playing, and believing in a happy, peaceful life. So we have to provide them with that life. They also have a cat named Zhorik. They drew him, too. :)

March 31, 5:49 p.m.

Some coffee shops have opened back up. People are soaking up the sun and having coffee and pastries. The men and women of Kharkiv try to treat the servicemen, who bashfully decline, but the men and women insist, so the lines move very slowly. :)

Some of them cry, overwhelmed with emotion, others embrace their friends, overjoyed to see them. It looks like Ukraine has just won the World Cup. :) At the edge of town are so many abandoned dogs; they look out of place and keep getting into fights. :(The city center got hit hard—we were standing nearby—and then there was some smoke. Nothing like that has happened for the past few days. :(

My friends and I went to an art exhibition by the brilliant Oleh Kalashnyk. It was an exhibition about the war; it was in the making for six months and the opening was on February 22. The ability of artists to detect what's most important is astounding.

We stopped by the Shevchenko Theatre, too, and congratulated them—the Berezil Theatre, Les Kurbas's great avant-garde troupe, was founded one hundred years ago today. :) The set hadn't been taken down—the final rehearsal of *Maklenka Grasa* was supposed to take place on February 24, and the premiere was slated for February 25. There you have it, history emerging in space. :(Sometimes it seems as though we all know each other's faces now. And I'll tell you, these are some damn pretty faces. :)

[. . .]

April 1, 7:38 a.m.

Our concert is today. :) The kids drew the poster for it. :) Naturally, I'd draw the insignia for the Armed Forces of Ukraine instead of a peace sign, but I still like the way they did it. :) Rise and shine, my friends, and let's work toward our victory. :)

The poster advertises, "Concert in the metro on April 1, 2022, 4:00 p.m."

April 1, 11:28 a.m.

We cleared out our destroyed studio. The building got hit hard, but our equipment and instruments are still alive and kicking. So we'll see another day and another song. :)

April 2, 9:20 a.m.

We held a concert for the wonderful kids staying in the Kharkiv metro. The kids sang, danced, and then they ate all the goodies we'd brought them. They've been doing creative activities and working with a psychologist and watching the kind of entertainers you'd hire for a birthday party. They're an organized, cheerful, and cohesive unit. :) They all sang the national anthem (and they even stuck to the official lyrics). :)

Good morning, dear brothers and sisters. I wish you all the best.

April 2, 11:32 a.m.

Kyrylo and Tymofiy are brothers. Kyrylo is twelve and Tymofiy is nine. They're responsible for the younger kids—they call them the munchkins :)—staying at two metro stations.

"What should we bring you?" I asked Tymofiy yesterday.

"Nothing," he said. Then he paused to think. "Actually, bring some rugs so the munchkins aren't crawling around on the cold floor."

Well, rugs it is! Gave the brothers an excuse to take a break from their homework, too. :)

Our kids grow fast, and they understand everything perfectly well. You don't have to explain to them who has come to their doorstep to wage war. The Russian world has nothing to offer them, and we will preserve the Ukrainian world for them. :)

April 3, 9:22 a.m.

I just visited my aunt, the amazing poet and translator Oleksandra Kovalyova. She's been in Kharkiv this whole time. She's been writing poems and staying upbeat. To a great extent it's thanks to her I started writing—I read her books and the books she recommended and showed her what I'd written. I love her so much. :)

April 3, 10:45 a.m.

Can't help but have strange feelings when coffee shops are opening back up in the city center while people are still hiding in basements on the eastern edge of town. We received an order. Sixteen people, all elderly, were hunkered down in a basement. We brought them some food. There are shredded clouds in the sky out toward Chuhuiv. It's springtime, but it's still chilly. Everyone wants sun, peace, and normalcy.

April 3, 7:36 p.m.

Let's stick together, my friends. All this truth that has stupefied us—the testimonies from Bucha—it's unbearable, of course. Indeed, this is why the Russians have come, to annihilate us. The only way for us to come out alive is to win this war. So let's work toward our victory and support the Armed Forces of Ukraine. We'll get to everything else afterward. For now, we have to resist, fight, and support each other. I'm speechless. Simply speechless. Hang in there, my friends. Tomorrow, we'll wake up one day closer to our victory.

April 4, 2:09 p.m.

The sky above Kharkiv is shrouded in heavy rain-clouds with the sharp, spring sun slicing through them. Looks like a flag left ragged by battle, snatched at by the wind. It's chilly in the morning; there aren't many people out, but later in the day there are more and more cars and pedestrians.

You can still bump into friends as you walk down the street, though. I just bumped into a buddy of mine who got a wolf and raccoons out of a wildlife sanctuary this morning. They came under machine-gun fire but made it out. Raccoons and all. :)

Time has become compressed; this ongoing misfortune feels like one day, leaving flashes in its wake: the chief of staff of a new unit that takes us from one address to another, the grandma who's buying two apples for 5.50 hryvnias at the store and is adamant about paying for herself, shredded fliers for an Ani Lorak concert, the siren that cuts out abruptly, and then the deep, inexhaustible silence that sets in.

It's springtime in the city, and the city is armed. Ukrainian flags flutter above the city.

April 4, 8:48 p.m.

Oh, yeah, yesterday, we held a real wedding ceremony for two of our volunteer doctors, Nastya and Anton. They're strong, radiant, courageous people who decided to counter all this darkness bearing down on us with their love. I wish them all the best. It was an honor to play for them. After the war is over, invite me to rock out at your wedding, now that I have some experience. :)

Sleep serenely, dear brothers and sisters. Tomorrow, we'll wake up one day closer to our victory.

April 5, 2:20 p.m.

It was sunny this morning, just some clouds drifting from over by Oleksiivka. In the afternoon, clouds covered the sky; however, you can still sense the presence of the sun, which gives the clouds a leaden tint. Basically, spring is here. :)

We hit some traffic for the first time today, and just a little over ten yards ahead of us, two cars—Ladas, by the way—crashed into each other in the middle of the intersection. I've already mentioned that there are a lot of old cars out on the roads. Well, two of them ran right into each other: the first driver slammed on the brakes, while the other one didn't. There was no traffic light. Basically, dear residents and guests of Kharkiv, be watchful and considerate of others on the road. :(

We delivered aid. They were surprised, yet happy to see us at the hospital. The women who work there speak cute Sloboda Ukrainian. :)

Stopped by a warehouse, too. A huge amount of aid is being brought here from all over the country, and then it gets delivered around the city. It's a kind of parallel structure, invisible yet powerful. We took a carload of groceries to a metro station. Some younger people ran out to help us unload them.

"Can we take a picture with you?" they asked.

"Nah," I said, "why don't I take a picture with you? I need it for my report."

Buildings in Zhuky were hit badly. They're all burnt out now. In Lyptsy, smoke rises into the sky. We stopped by to see our boys. A shell landed nearby and wrecked their minivan two days ago. The whole body is full of shrapnel. We're going to repair it.

A volunteer traffic cop stood on one of the bridges between the cinder blocks. :) He directs traffic, waving his arms confidently, if not completely soberly. He's stopping a lot of jeeps. :) I met with the regional government.

"So," I asked, "what do you think about the city coming under attack?"

"They won't be able to pull it off," they said wearily, yet confidently.

Servicemen order decaf at coffee shops. Ukrainian troops are Europeans, aesthetes. It's windy in the city. Ukrainian flags flutter above the city. :)

April 5, 9:24 p.m.

Walking around the city in the evening is strange. Not too many people are out, but everyone's got a dog, and they're all walking them at once. :) Everyone's getting ready for curfew and bed. The overblown rumors of an upcoming offensive haven't really seemed to scare anyone. We're in our city. We're home. The Armed Forces of Ukraine are with us. :)

Sweet dreams, dear brothers and sisters. Have a quiet night. Tomorrow, we'll wake up one day closer to our victory. :)

April 6, 7:14 a.m.

I met up with my friends. In their past, prewar lives, they were activists and volunteers from Kharkiv. They did a lot for the city. Now they're all fighting. We bumped into each other in town: some of them had come straight from the front and were taking care of military business, while others just had some free time. We spoke on the phone and decided to hang out together for a few hours. Even ordered pizza. :)

Since the first day of the war, we'd only crossed paths by chance—around town or at a checkpoint. So we all wanted to talk, get it all out, pour out these new, bitter, and trying experiences. None of them are professional soldiers, so they had to learn by taking up arms and going into battle in the very first days. That's precisely what they spoke about: their initial fear, disappointment, first victories, suspicions, and the exhilaration they felt because our forces are holding their ground. Every one of them has his own story, every one of them is eager, in such a hurry, to tell it, seemingly afraid he'll forget something. They don't listen to each other all that closely. Right now, they all just need to get it out. What emerges from all this is a strange multitude of men's voices, a rising generation of men who took up arms to defend their country. Weapons, dark and cold, lie right in the middle of the room. And the pizza is cold, too. Nobody's eating, everyone's talking. You can't get it all out now, though: there are still many stories and voices up ahead, the war is up ahead. What matters most is that they're all still alive and healthy. And their weapons are at their sides. :) Good morning, my friends.

April 6, 7:44 a.m.

Friends in different countries, everyone who supports Ukraine today and everyone who is watching this tragedy unfolding in the middle of Europe, I'd like you to understand one basic thing—we appreciate every word of support, every gesture of solidarity, and this really is important to us. But what Ukrainians need more than anything in order to survive and keep being Ukrainian is weapons. The Russians are committing genocide against us. They have come here to annihilate us. There is no political or military justification for their actions. They are war criminals. Rest assured, they will be held responsible for their crimes. But today, we need to defend ourselves and win. And to do that, we need weapons. I suspect that our friends the Poles understand our situation better than anyone else. Back in 1944, during the Warsaw Uprising, that's exactly what they needed—weapons. Weapons that provide protection and a chance at a future. Put pressure on your parliaments. Put pressure on your representatives who will try to talk about geopolitical expediency and economic benefits. A Ukrainian defeat in this war will be a defeat for the whole civilized world. Contrarily, a Ukrainian victory will be a testament to the fact that honor, conscience, and responsibility still carry weight in the world. We need weapons!

April 6, 11:18 a.m.

Kharkiv's hills prop up the sky. In the distance, newly built apartment complexes crowd together with clouds scattered overhead. The skies are fresh and fluid.

In the forest park, spring feels particularly deep and sharp. Yet the volleys sound especially hollow and voluminous. We delivered aid to some doctors and agreed to stay in touch.

Tremendous work is being done around the clock at warehouses: the workers receive aid from across the country, repackage it, and deliver it all over the city.

Servicemen occasionally reach out, but they always request specific things that address particular needs. You can sense that the city is armed, and that our servicemen are charged up, thanks, in part, to volunteers. It's a nice realization.

There was pizza for sale at the supermarket. We eyed it, thought for a second, and then bought lots of freshly baked bread: for ourselves, for the doctors, and some for the elderly people we've been helping out. Spring seeps through the city. Ukrainian flags flutter above the city.

April 6, 1:15 p.m.

I visited my dog, Barik. What a beast! :) He's from Luhansk—been through a lot. Several years ago, I got him and my mom out of the Luhansk Region, away from the war. Barik quickly adapted to his new circumstances in Kharkiv, started to feel young again, and was living it up. The war caught up to him here, though. He was afraid and depressed when the shelling started. But then spring came, it got a little warmer, and he came back to life. Although he does really miss everyone. These days, pets are in dire need of peace and quiet and their usual comforts. Just like everyone else. We'll adjust back to our normal lives after we win. Look after each other, dear brothers and sisters. :)

April 7, 6:04 p.m.

We just performed for our boys. First time performing for our servicemen since the beginning.

Since 2014, we've put on hundreds of concerts for servicemen, from Stanytsia Luhanska to Chonhar. Each time, you could tell they were full of special emotions, special conversations, and special things.

But now you look at the boys after forty days of fighting, and you realize just how different everything is. The fighters are like steel glowing from within: wrathful, strong, formidable. Entirely different voices, a different glint in their eyes. They even sing the anthem differently. :) Like a hymn. There are a lot of people I know, a lot of them would come to concerts before the war.

They had quite a bit of interesting stuff to say. Unfortunately, I can't tell you everything. Some of them had just gotten out of the hospital and returned to duty. No fear whatsoever; no fatigue whatsoever. Everyone's staying where he should be, protecting the city, bearing arms. The people make up our forces. :)

We also saw a car being repaired at the edge of town. Kharkiv is incorrigible. I mean that in a good way, though. :) Have a calm, quiet night, dear brothers and sisters. Let Ukrainian flags flutter above our cities. Tomorrow, we'll wake up one day closer to our victory. :)

April 8, 11:41 a.m.

A good friend of mine, the great tennis player Serhiy Stakhovsky, just stopped by. These days, he's a fighter, a warrior. We talked, shared what we knew, and hit the court. Kharkiv has been under bombardment since last evening, including parts of the city that haven't been hit before. The city isn't frightened, though—just wary, more than anything. Everyone realizes that they may come under fire, but they have to do their jobs. As the servicemen said yesterday, "We won't give up the city, but be careful." So we're all being careful. And dear brothers and sisters, please be careful—we've got children to raise and cities to rebuild. Wishing you all the best.

April 8, 1:35 p.m.

I remember going to Kramatorsk in December 2013. I went to their Maidan demonstration. Seven or eight people gathered by the Shevchenko monument. They gathered every day, despite all the pressure they faced. After that, in 2014, Kramatorsk became dear to me. Since then, we've performed there a hundred times: at libraries, schools, military bases, clubs. We've delivered books and spoken with local teachers. We'd often pick up friends in Kyiv who went there by train, hopped on our bus, and then rolled down the roads of the Donbas. Last time we stopped at the train station was in January— we were waiting for our cameraman, sitting there, people watching. Now you look at the footage from the Kramatorsk train station and you're speechless. How could anyone do something like that? How could anyone wage war like that? Russian soldiers have no conscience, no dignity. Trash, utter trash.

April 8, 7:04 p.m.

These days, people in town can be divided into two distinct categories: those who have found themselves in these circumstances and those who haven't. It seems to hit men particularly hard—like when a grown man, self-assured and successful before the war, is hunkering down with old ladies, waiting for volunteers to bring them canned food. Or when a man is walking down the street and you see that his eyes are empty. :(

I'm writing this without any grievances or reproach, though. We're all different, and there's no point demanding what we aren't capable of. More than anything, this is just a sad reminder of the havoc this war is wreaking on us . . .

Besides that, flocks fly above Kharkiv—they're returning from their wintering grounds and trying to figure out what has happened here, what has changed. We're glad to have them. A few weeks ago, there was nothing flying over the city but Russian bombers. I unexpectedly found myself at a jazz concert. :) The brilliant Serhiy Davydov and his friends put on a fantastic three-hour show at one of the clubs in town. They sounded tender, heart wrenching; I got to listening and thinking about the sheer number of brilliant people in our city, about what an amazing place it is. :)

It's been a quiet spring evening. The sky is high and damp. Sometimes it starts drizzling. Then it lets up, and the smell of dust daintily dots the air. Our anti-aircraft weapons sound like April thunder—just as loud and life affirming. :) And I'll say it again, just so you don't have any doubt—Ukrainian flags flutter above the city. :)

Rest up, my friends. Tomorrow, we'll wake up one day closer to our victory.

April 9, 12:06 p.m.

It's sunny and brisk in the morning, birds' chirping can be heard on the city's sidewalks and fat cats drowsily soak up the sun on car hoods.

You can't help but notice that the tram tracks are all rusty from lack of use. Pedestrians flag down cars and ask for rides. A lot of people have taken up bike riding. :) I saw a guy carting his wife around in a car seat.

Zhuky is quiet and anxious. There's a spring wind in the forest park. As usual, there's smoke above Saltivka. :(

Got a call from the Moskovskiy District. Ten retirees asking for something, anything. We brought them some aid.

The Karazin University administration joined us to stop by a hospital and drop off some vitamins. :) I'll write a separate post about the university. We spoke to the head doctor. He's a top-notch specialist. He told us a lot of stories. Most of them weren't all that cheerful—they were about wounded civilians, women, and children. :(

We're rolling again, going to look for an armored vehicle for one of our units. You constantly find yourself thinking that there are so many strong, luminous people in this city. The city exudes spring. Ukrainian flags flutter above the city. :)

April 9, 8:10 p.m.

A residential building on Otakar Jaroš Street in Kharkiv just got hit. The Russians continue to annihilate Ukrainians simply because they're Ukrainians. The city is being terrorized, but it stopped being afraid a long time ago. For those who have stayed and are well aware where they've decided to stay, they will have a lot of work to do tomorrow. And the day after. And then we'll win and start rebuilding our schools, hospitals, and universities.

Rest up, my friends. We have to stay strong and keep our wits about us. :) Tomorrow, we'll wake up one day closer to our victory.

April 11, 11:29 a.m.

Come morning, you can hear outgoing artillery fire in the air. You look at the sky and try to discern something, anything, but it's so high up there, dotted with light spring clouds. And when the thundering abates, spring pounces with all its smells, with all its sun and dust. In the park, municipal workers are planting something. The park is well maintained; fresh trash bags hang on the trees. Can't help but notice that everyone has grown accustomed to these new circumstances—most passersby pay no mind to the outgoing fire. The 125th foreign TV company films the Shevchenko monument as municipal workers stack sandbags around it for the fifth time—they keep singing. :) Looks like Mr. Shevchenko is bursting out of the bags so he can see everything for himself. :) And nobody pays any mind to the guys with guns running into the supermarket to pick up some milk. Overall, despite the constant booming sounds overhead, the city center is somewhat calm. It's hard to say the same about the eastern edge of the city, where there was fighting. Over there, it looks like the land itself has been turned upside down. :(

Aside from that, life goes on in Kharkiv. Restaurants are starting to open back up. The city is cleaning up and gunning up. Ukrainian flags flutter above the city.

April 11, 5:06 p.m.

I've always enjoyed talking about Kharkiv as a city of students. I don't really care for the conceptualizations of Kharkiv that have gained official support since the nineties—"the first capital," "the cultural capital." Generally, I didn't care for this attempt to juxtapose it with Kyiv. Kharkiv, the city of students—now that's a definition I find appealing and productive. Several hundred thousand young faces and voices around have made this city truly special. I've spoken with folks at a bunch of different universities. Mostly at my alma mater, Skovoroda Kharkiv National Pedagogical University, naturally, but I've also done work with Karazin University. I remember when Yaroslav Markevych and I established the Fifth Kharkiv and tons of people came to our cultural events.

I remember being awarded an honorary doctorate degree by the folks at Karazin.

The chancellor asked, her voice hopeful, "You aren't going to put on the cap and gown, are you?"

"Now why wouldn't I?" I replied.

The cap and gown were silly, but it was nice to wear them. :) I remember sitting down with the chancellor afterward and talking about establishing a robust cultural and educational center on the old university campus that would stretch for a whole block. And we also agreed to put a commemorative plaque for George Shevelov on the wall of the building where he worked. We didn't get a chance to do it, though.

During the first days of the bombardment, I remember bumping into a group of Indian students on Klochkivska Street. Eyes filled with terror, they were trying to escape to the train station. The girl leading the pack was running and holding an Indian flag, like it was a totem or talisman of sorts. These days, Kharkiv's universities are empty. Karazin has lost its athletic complex, dormitories, and their buildings in Piatykhatky. The main building stands, albeit with shattered windows. But the university administration and I met the other day to talk about our problems, about ways to solve them, and about education in general.

The official reason was to kick off an auction. Maryna Lytovchenko, a graduate of Karazin and a Paralympic champion, auctioned off her gold medals to raise funds for the university. The unofficial reason was to make sure everyone was alive and well. And that instruction was continuing. I mean education is, first and foremost, about the future. And our future is a city of intelligent, skilled, and educated citizens who love their country.

I really do want students to return to the classroom as quickly as possible at my dear alma mater Skovoroda, at Karazin, now also dear to me, and at all of Kharkiv's other universities. And they will. Because we Ukrainians love studying and value knowledge. :)

April 11, 8:44 p.m.

In the afternoon, a rocket landed not too far from the city center (actually, I know exactly where, but I shouldn't say). Smoke rose high and dark into the sky. It feels like the battle for the city is taking place overhead, above us. Things are booming up there, things are flying up there. Sometimes something falls to the ground. :(

And I've caught myself thinking that we're constantly finding, ordering, and purchasing all sorts of stuff for our troops. These days, all of this is found, paid for, and redirected to Kharkiv. A lot of amazing people have been helping Kharkiv. In other words, the city is getting even stronger and better equipped to resist. Time is on our side. We just have to remember that and not succumb to despair. We have something worth fighting for. And people to do the fighting.

Quiet dreams, dear brothers and sisters. Tomorrow, we'll wake up one day closer to our victory.

April 12, 12:12 p.m.

Today, Ukrainian Post released a stamp about the Russian warship. We attended the unveiling in Kharkiv and bought a bunch of envelopes so we can write to our relatives in Russia. I mean, everyone from Kharkiv has relatives in Russia, right? :)

Jokes aside, my friends—remember to write or call your loved ones. It's really important to support each other these days. You can send handwritten letters. Ukrainian Post will deliver them in their wonderful new envelopes. :)

(*Sideways on left*): "First Day"; (*postage stamp*): "Ukraine"; (*stamped text below postage stamp*): "Russian Warship, Go . . . !, Kharkiv, 010652, April 12, 2022"; (*bottom*): "Russian Warship, Go . . . !"

April 13, 6:23 p.m.

As far as you can tell from the news, the bombardment of Kharkiv is getting more intense. But you can't feel that when you're racing around town. Drove over to Bavaria—things are quiet and subdued. Drove over to Blahbaz—just another day at the market. Even Baraban was full of life. The sky came alive with noise as soon as we got there, though. Pole was quiet, Zhuky and Moskalivka, too. Then we returned to our home base, and black smoke was hovering up in the sky at the spot we'd just come from. You read the news—Zhuky is under bombardment. That's just what I was writing about yesterday—about the chimerical, tenuous nature of danger and vulnerability. These days, the whole city is a potential target. And the worst thing is that it's mostly civilians getting killed. Someone going outside to get some fresh air. Someone who decided to go for a walk with their kid. For the Russians, we're all targets. They don't care whether we're armed or not—they're annihilating us simply because we're here, because we live here, because we're Ukrainian.

Aside from that, it was a productive day. We loaded up a car with humanitarian aid, which we'll deliver tomorrow. Our wonderful friends (the cultural institution Mizhbukvamy and a magnificent person nicknamed Ray) shared their tourniquets and other useful things with us, and we immediately sent them to our units.

Then our stalker Oleh the Pyrotechnician arrived from Dnipro with a huge truck packed with things for our servicemen. :) And that's when the real action started. But it's worth writing a separate post about that.

It's windy in Kharkiv, tempestuous even. The wind whips at our flags, but it can't tear them down. :) Because they're our flags. They keep fluttering above our city.

Have a nice—and preferably quiet—evening. Conserve your energy and emotion. We have to hold out and win. Tomorrow, we'll wake up one day closer to our victory. :)

April 14, 7:39 a.m.

Kharkiv kids who are abroad are missing their hometown and singing folk songs. :) I really want them all to return home as quickly as possible so Kharkiv's streets can be crowded with young people again. These days, Kharkiv is stronger than ever, but it's a little empty. When everyone comes back, it'll warm up and get a new song.

Good morning, my friends. Rise and shine. Let's get to work.

April 14, 10:26 p.m.

You can sense that everyone feels the need to get everything out, to say what's filling them up, what makes them who they are. We're looking for our own words, grasping for our own intonation. Words often betray us in these circumstances, which jerk us around wildly; the situation is too painful. At any rate, it's important to maintain our right to speak. As well as our ability to listen. We'll find common ground. We just have to win— that's what matters most.

Have a quiet night, my friends. Tomorrow, we'll wake up one day closer to our victory.

P.S. The photograph is of a performance by Slava Vakarchuk and Kharkiv musicians in the demolished courtyard of the Palace of Labor.

April 16, 8:16 p.m.

Today was such a long day. In the morning, we drove one of the cars and dropped it off with the boys. We saw what they were wearing, so we gave them our four bulletproof vests. We won't be needing them, but they could come in handy where our boys are. We cut through the city and popped out beyond the outer ring road, and spring was in full swing there. We've got friends at checkpoints, volunteer centers, administrative buildings, and gas stations. :) The city has turned into a powerful horizontal system of smooth coordination and assistance.

In the evening we held an event for the children in one of the metro stations—we put on a puppet show and brought them some treats. The children are bright-eyed and courageous everywhere, but, damn, they don't need this experience, not one bit. :(

Kharkiv is as strong as ever. Big and strong. The city is inhaling fresh wind. It's being bombarded, but it can't be destroyed. And notice how pretty our flags are in this April light. :)

Rest up, my friends. Tomorrow, we'll wake up one day closer to our victory.

April 18, 10:28 a.m.

In the morning, I got word of the street fighting in Kreminna. I recalled going to the lyceum there when we were holding Read-Write, a youth language arts competition. The kids and teachers were great, always taking part in talent shows and academic competitions, winning and receiving awards.

I have a sharp, distinct childhood memory: my dad and I are driving through Kreminna on our way home, and he buys me a set of toy soldiers and a little tank at the local department store. :) For some reason, I still remember that tank. Now there are real tanks in the city. All I can do is hope that the students and their teachers are safe. It's clear that this Holy Week will be a tough one, my friends. Stick together, put your trust in the Armed Forces of Ukraine, and take care of each other. We have to withstand this, and we have to rebuild our schools and libraries. Everything will be all right, everything will be Ukraine.

[. . .]

April 19, 8:41 p.m.

These days, the way the Ukrainianness of people in Kharkiv soaks through everything can be truly stunning. I'm not just referring to the Ukrainian language. I mean their Ukrainian stance. And their use of language, too.

When a middle-aged woman selling a train ticket to an old lady, or a man at the market making axes for tank drivers, or a woman picking out balaclavas for our fighters all speak insanely natural (though not entirely grammatical) Ukrainian, it indicates that they are with us, that they support Ukraine.

Despite all the blood and pain, some significant shifts are taking place in the city. And I wouldn't want that all to disappear after we regain control over our borders.

Also, it's disheartening when you realize that we've lost an awful lot of time and resources over the past thirty years. I mean, all these men and women were born here, Ukrainians in Ukrainian Kharkiv, but they had to be reduced to percentage points in someone's electoral games. All I can do is hope that we'll learn something from today's carnage. Rest up, dear brothers and sisters. Tomorrow, we'll wake up one day closer to our victory.

April 20, 1:19 p.m.

It's all clouds and rain in Kharkiv. There are as many cars out as there were before; pedestrians wear raincoats. The city quickly bounced back after the bombardment in the center. Yesterday, a little street market was set up right by the building that got hit. Folks ask each other what places are open, where they can get some groceries or a haircut.

The volunteers are still working to get equipment to our forces. These days, you can't help but notice it—all the aid for the army, that is: everyone trades equipment,

shares what they have, and gives out contact information for those who can deliver something.

This morning, we received a ton of very durable
shoes from Solomiia Bobrovska and sent them to a Territorial Defense unit. A different unit got tactical goggles, underwear, and a thermal imager.

Vitalik Selyk brought a big pile of meds from Kyiv. Aid
keeps coming in from all over the country.

The city is alive, a little battered, but full of spring and
rain. Ukrainian flags flutter above the city. :)

April 20, 2:43 p.m.

We got an old lady out of North Saltivka. She had a
charming, old-time Sloboda Ukraine way of speaking.
Her relatives found themselves in occupied territory.
She was struggling, so we took her to a safe place.

She shared her experience of surviving the shelling.

"Lots of rumbling last night. Just like the day before
that. And the day before that," she said, "there I am,
walking back from the store when one landed right at
my feet. And everyone's yelling at me, 'Get down.' And I
ask them, 'If I get down, will you pick me up?'"

"Whose guns am I hearing?" she asks, reacting to the
sounds. "Ours?"

"Ours," we reply.

"Ours . . . that's a good thing," she said. "Then every-thing's nice and calm."

Most Ukrainians call humanitarian aid *huminitarka,* but she says *humatarka.* She complained that no one had come to help.

"I mean," she said, "I wasn't actually looking for any-thing, but nobody was delivering anything either."

Eighty years old, two strokes under her belt. "Like a bunch of cockroaches"—that's what she had to say about the Russians. These days, old people are particu-larly helpless and disoriented. I feel bad for them, really do. They just can't get by without us. Take care of each other, my friends. These days, having a big heart really matters.

[. . .]

April 20, 9:11 p.m.

Kharkiv is being bombarded again. They just won't leave this city alone. Meanwhile, everything is in bloom, filling up with warmth. It's disheartening that the enemy is taking our lives, our time, and our resources away. But we'll rebuild everything. This is our city. We love it. Have a quiet evening, my friends. Tomorrow, we'll wake up one day closer to our victory.

April 21, 3:16 p.m.

Stopped by a children's party this morning. My friend Valeriy gave the kids a ton of candy. We chatted, read some poems, and talked about who had what kind of cat. :)

My dear friend Katya Kalytko arrived, bringing some humanitarian aid for our center, and most important—

yes, these days this is what's truly most important—she brought a bunch of useful things for our unit: two thermal imagers, night binoculars, two day-and-night-vision scopes, two silencers, ballistic eyewear, backpacks for rocket-propelled grenades, cartridge pouches, and load-bearing vests. As well as sleeping bags, mats, and canned goods for our fighters.

We greeted our heroic "brass section"—as Ukrainian infantrymen have taken to calling themselves. :) Sasha and Artem passed along a large box of meds and a scope with a tripod for the snipers in one of our units.

Put it to good use, boys. :) I had a meeting with Yulia Laputina, the minister of veterans' affairs. We spoke about the future of the ministry, about psychological rehabilitation for veterans, and about what has been transpiring in the territory we've recently liberated.

We held a concert to raise funds for one of Kharkiv's units. Lots of my friends who have been combining volunteering with their creative pursuits, to the extent that's possible in times like these.

We also have a meeting coming up with a group of Americans who are shooting a movie about Kharkiv, and this evening's cultural program includes visiting some artists' studios. Kharkiv's painters and sculptors have kept working. Because there isn't any other way, is there?

Actually, I wanted to say that people in town are always getting word of a possible storm or a probable offensive by the enemy. The city isn't afraid, though. And it never has been afraid, since the very beginning. We have our love and our armed forces. :) That's enough to believe and not be afraid.

There's wind, sun, and clouds above the city. Ukrainian flags flutter above the city. :)

April 22, 11:36 a.m.

I've noticed this one thing—these days, the landscape of the city, its substance, its structure has a completely different feel to it.

When you venture into this or that neighborhood, you immediately recall whether it's been hit or not, and if it has been, you recall the last time it was. This perception of the city, driven by the war, is completely different—distinguishing neighborhoods by their potential threat level and the degree of damage done. I have to say this is a rather joyless way of perceiving where you live.

I think we'll continue to see our city like this for a long time after the war—this place got hit, this one didn't, thank God. Then this whole optical system will erode away to nothing, that's obvious. That's the way it ought to be. Here in Kharkiv, we aren't very well aware of what particular city blocks were hammered the hardest in August and September 1943. Now looking at the city hurts. You want to protect it. Which is just what the Armed Forces of Ukraine are doing. :) And we're helping out a little. :)

Besides that, Kharkiv is sunny. Ukrainian flags flutter above Kharkiv. :)

April 22, 8:39 p.m.

In the afternoon, it's calm and quiet in the city center. All of this clashes with the news about the post office and mall being hit by Russian artillery. There are fewer people out, but still lots of cars.

The city is green and cloudy, somewhat solemn even. That may be because Easter is just around the corner. You walk down the streets and you keep bumping into volunteers who are hauling something or other from a warehouse, loading cars, sorting their cargo, and moving out. Today, we got a bunch of useful stuff, procured some things, and made some arrangements. I'll give you more details tomorrow. :)

There were a lot of foreign journalists at a coffee shop in town, like it was a bona fide press club or something. :) These days, a lot of European media outlets have been coming to Kharkiv—as well they should—we must give the world a chance to talk about this war. These days, Russia is a global problem, so the world simply doesn't have the moral right to ignore what's going on in our backyard. Besides that, a siren begins blaring, this heavy, alarming sound hollows the air out, and spring no longer seems all that carefree.

The city lives on, hangs on, and defends itself. Rest up, dear brothers and sisters—tomorrow, we'll wake up one day closer to our victory. :)

April 23, 11:43 a.m.

My friends, I'd like to address my readers who aren't citizens of Ukraine. Just spoke to the boys defending Mariupol. They're certain that there's still a chance to evacuate the defenders of the city, women, children, and the wounded, first and foremost.

You all know what the situation has been in Mariupol. You all see the Russians annihilating the people at the Azovstal plant. The defenders of the city have been calling upon the international community to put pressure on the Russian government to establish an evacuation corridor for those who are currently at Azovstal.

We can't let hundreds of people, including civilians, get wiped out. Every effort has to be made to save them. We still have a chance to do so. Put pressure on your governments, spread the word. Mariupol needs the world's support.

April 23, 3:44 p.m.

We blessed several hundred paskas—traditional Easter bread—and then delivered them to two metro stations. Everyone should be able to celebrate, regardless of whether they have the opportunity to go to church or if it's more advisable to stay underground. :) The children were particularly pleased. And when children are happy, adults feel good. :)

My heartfelt appreciation goes out to Dmytro Kutoviy. Take care of each other, dear brothers and sisters. :)

April 24, 8:37 a.m.

Christ is risen, dear believers and agnostics! Wishing you health and happiness! :)

April 24, 9:52 p.m.

We went to see the boys in Chuhuiv. The road was empty. Chuhuiv itself is quiet and green. We got there right after a bombardment. There's talk of three wounded. :(Youngsters have set up a children's checkpoint on one of the streets in town. They're playing war.

We brought the boys some blessed paskas, various treats, and some other things. They're local boys from Kharkiv, Chuhuiv, or Malynivka. They told us a lot of interesting stuff about the first days of the war, about how the locals' attitudes and feelings toward Russia had changed. Returning to Kharkiv is like entering a fortress. And these days, that's exactly what it is.

Right before curfew, we managed to buy a Jeep for the boys posted outside of Izium: found an ad on the internet, showed up, checked it, paid up, and rolled out. :) Thanks to everyone who has been helping out. These days, every penny goes toward our victory. Rain came in the early evening. Cloudy spring. Ukrainian flags flutter above the city. :)

Rest up, my friends. Tomorrow, we'll wake up one day closer to our victory.

P.S. In the photograph, a priest is speaking to our fighters about Christ, about how you can cross paths or miss him. There are three flags on the wall: Ukrainian, American, and Ukrainian Insurgent Army. You could say these are three aspects of our fight: our statehood, our allies, and our memory, which makes us stronger. :)

April 25, 6:18 p.m.

Our friendly crew took three carloads of useful things to Zolochiv for a unit that was recently posted there. Before that, we spent a good half of the day collecting saws–axes–construction staples–shovels–hygiene products. We bought some stuff ourselves, and our friends from Kharkiv's boundless community of volunteers chipped in some stuff, too.

In the villages outside the city, spring has arrived—that's for sure. It's quiet and green. Old ladies sit on benches, cows graze in meadows, and geese gingerly march along the road. There's some machinery in the fields here and there—agricultural machinery, that is. And black smoke hovering on the horizon, in the direction of the border.

Incoming and outgoing fire was humming constantly in town, so we unloaded everything and then headed straight home. :(I couldn't help noticing a schoolboy walking with determination down the main street, looking like this war had nothing to do with him. We shared our chocolate and wished him luck. :) Black smoke looms over several areas of Kharkiv, but it's still nice to return to the city. It's evening in the city. Ukrainian flags flutter above the city.

April 25, 8:35 p.m.

The country's quiet after Easter.

Rivers trickle slowly.

Christians and fools meekly bring glory to the
Lord.

An exchange as warm as a lantern.

You never know who your enemy is.

The sky's as quiet as a hospital

whose patients have been evacuated.

Someone has opened the air's core.

Dark forests—places for choristers.

A valiant fight for faith in Christ

being waged by a country of agnostics and
atheists.

Women holding mirrors like icons.

The mirrors have portents only they can see.

Things will never be as they are now.

Things can only be this way in April.

2020

Rest up, dear brothers and sisters. Tomorrow, we'll
wake up one day closer to our victory.

April 26, 9:40 a.m.

Just yesterday evening, smoke was drifting from the
west, coming from the outer ring road, yet come morn-

ing, clear skies hung high over the city, with light weight-
less clouds here and there. I noticed that the paths in the
park near the Naukova metro station, well-trodden last
year, have become somewhat overgrown—there are, indeed, fewer people in the city. This reminds me of what
Kharkiv was like in August back in the nineties, before
all the students had come back, when you mostly saw
older people out and about.

A church courtyard, red with tulips. It smells in-
tensely of apple blossoms. Someone is feeding pigeons
under a balcony. They flock in great numbers and peck
intently.

Dogs race cheerfully across the fresh grass. It's a
quiet morning. In the city center, at least. Day 62 of the
war. Good morning, everyone.

April 26, 8:03 p.m.

Dear residents of the Kherson Region. I know that
the occupiers would like to hold a pseudo-referendum
tomorrow. I'd like to address everyone who follows this
page and give you an obvious reminder. We haven't forgotten about you. Ukraine will return shortly. Don't give
up and don't be afraid! For those who aren't afraid, here
is some information regarding tactical action that can
be taken:

[. . .]

Share this and take action! Everything will be all
right, everything will be Ukraine!

Take action while you are under occupation!

The occupiers have no place on your land. Tell
them that anywhere you can.

They've come to "liberate" you. Show them they
aren't welcome here.

Fasten flags and yellow ribbons anywhere people
might see them!

If you don't have a flag or ribbons, find old yellow
clothes and cut them into little strips. Hang
up the yellow strips where everyone can see
them: on road signs, railings, door handles,
bus stops, pipes, and trees. Just remember
that we haven't forgotten about you and we
never will! The Armed Forces of Ukraine will
drive the occupiers out of your homes and return your land to Ukraine.

Glory to Ukraine!

#YellowRibbon #KhersonisUkraine

April 28, 8:00 p.m.

Ukrainian Action gave us a wonderful pickup that we
shipped off to our unit right away. Thanks, my friends.
You can't imagine how much we needed it—and how perfectly timed its arrival was. :)

We brought the boys a ton of other stuff, too: a thermal imager, uniforms, jacks for their cars, sleeping bags, and thermal underwear. Ours is a people's army—an army truly supported by the people. :)

In the early evening, folks with dogs are out on Kharkiv's streets, walking their beasts. :) The city is empty, green, warm. The city has a terrible lack of movement and voices. But there's no lack of energy, that's for sure. :)

Rest up, my friends. Tomorrow, we'll wake up one day closer to our victory.

May 1, 8:08 p.m.

If you go visit some volunteers and fighters, you're bound to see bulletproof vests right next to the shoes people take off before they come inside—these are the strange realities of war.

We spoke to some volunteers who got people out of North Saltivka during the first few days. They told us a lot of stories, both funny and sad. We all have completely different experiences that we carry with us from these past sixty days: bombardments, evacuations, fallen friends, liberated towns. We all try to share these experiences. These voices are strong, confident, infused with spring air and anger. Not fatigue, though.

Have a quiet evening, my friends. Tomorrow, we'll wake up one day closer to our victory. :)

May 2, 11:27 a.m.

The Kharkiv National University of Arts is celebrating 105 years since its founding. Classes are online; roughly 80 percent of the professors have remained in Kharkiv.

The main building got hit pretty badly—a wave of explosions damaged a lot of the windows. Melancholy pianos withstood below-freezing temperatures in the classrooms. :) But now guests have come, and the music is playing. :)

The thing is, Kharkiv feels orphaned without culture, without theaters, without libraries, and without students. But all of that will come back, all of that will be rebuilt. Kharkiv's halls await their audiences. :)

May 2, 3:21 p.m.

In the morning, clouds hover low over the city. The air is brisk, and it feels like spring, but the streets are empty. There are cars racing about, though—too fast, Kharkiv-style.

The park smells sharply and keenly of freshly cut grass. A couple stands by the monument to opera singer Hulak-Artemovs'kyi. The young man reads the nineteenth-century writer's name out loud but pronounces it like "Artyom," the Soviet revolutionary who wouldn't come around until a hundred years later. :) Looks like visitors to the city are getting used to the new names. :)

Municipal workers paint little fences at intersections. There's plenty of greenery and few pedestrians in the city. Women walk down the street. One of them orders a long list of meds loudly over the phone. Over these past two months meds are everywhere, it turns out, people need so many.

Then the sun comes out. Things are more translucent, calmer, or something like that. Somebody takes pictures of tulips in Shevchenko Garden, somebody else walks purposefully to fill empty bottles with water. We gave our servicemen a couple of thermal imagers and one awesome little flying thing. Our dear friend Oleh the Pyrotechnician hauled in yet another generator and gave it to our unit—I suspect it won't be the last.

It's almost curfew—this is a wonderful time to get some work done. Spring has come to the city. Ukrainian flags flutter above the city.

Thank you all for the support.

May 2, 6:44 p.m.

We went to see the boys outside the city, brought them some groceries and hygiene products. It's remarkably quiet in the village. Hardly any of the locals are left. Those who remain have been helping each other out one way or another. No stores are open, no service, though.

The boys told us about how they helped put out the fires caused by Russian Grad rockets. They also told us about how the Russians agreed to let them send a column of vehicles out to evacuate the locals over to our side. Then they unleashed their Grad rockets on them. One woman got hit in the head and a fragment went straight through a boy's leg. Fortunately, they're all still alive. And fortunately, our boys are all alive and well. Debris, craters, and metal litter everything in the vicinity, though. Like somebody was digging around in the earth for a while but didn't find anything.

The early evening was quiet, yet something over the hill would tremble occasionally. Atop the hill, the whole horizon is shrouded in smoke, while tractor drivers work in the fields. Have a quiet evening, dear brothers and sisters. Take care of each other. Tomorrow, we'll wake up one day closer to our victory.

May 3, 8:53 p.m.

We dropped by one of the hospitals in the city and had a concert for the doctors and patients. Some of them haven't left the campus for over a month. So they asked us to swing by and show our support.

The experiences that the people of Kharkiv have gone through together these past two months are completely unprecedented—not at all joyful, yet real and honest.

It isn't even about politics or patriotism—it's about this feeling of finding your people, those whom you trust, whom you can rely on. I hope to God we'll be able to preserve this feeling of trust and mutual support after we win.

I realize that this wasn't a quiet evening for Ukraine, my friends. But I hope you are all alive and well and that you will feel strong and confident come morning.

Tomorrow, we'll wake up one day closer to our victory.

May 4, 9:07 a.m.

We had an online talk with my colleagues from the Skovoroda Kharkiv National Pedagogical University the other day. It was really nice to see the chancellor, professors, and students. Everyone misses face-to-face interactions terribly. Of course, no monitors, Zoom, or on-line events can fully compensate for them. Nonetheless, it was really nice. :)

Since we are all teachers—whether we're veterans or rookies :)—we spoke about the field of education and the work of teachers, particularly in small towns and villages, particularly in eastern Ukraine. I instantly re-called the dozens of stories I had the chance to hear from teachers in the Kharkiv, Luhansk, and Donetsk re-gions over the past eight years, the dozens of schools I visited, worked with, and supported financially.

I found myself thinking, "How much labor, love, and inspiration have teachers, the government, and volun-teers invested? How much were we able to offer them? How engaged were the teachers and students? How many interesting and dynamic changes did the field of education see during these eight years?" A lot of these schools have been leveled. Now everything that has been accomplished by thousands of creative, intelligent people deeply invested in their work is simply being de-stroyed.

The occupiers are putting Lenin monuments back up and imposing the Russian national curriculum. In other words, they're making a conscious and dogged attempt to drag us back into the past, to stop time, to replay his-tory. This is a kind of unfathomable and suicidal long-ing for timelessness and the other world. This longing isn't just suicidal, though—they're dragging us back into the past, too.

The only difference is that they seem to find this crusade into the past enchanting. We've had no use for it for the past hundred years, though. Because we've already done our hundred years since we lost our statehood. We can take care of it from here. And we'll rebuild our schools, that's for sure. Without Lenin, Gorky, or Kobzon. :)

Good morning from Kharkiv, my friends. It's sunny in these parts. Sirens wail now and then, but the sky is a sublime light blue. Look at the pretty flag above the city.

May 4, 12:12 p.m.

We met with the management at Ukrainian Railways. We've been in touch since the beginning of the war: constantly receiving things, greeting folks, or sending them off. We'd like to show our support for the railroad workers after yesterday's rocket attacks. They do a commendable job; they're real heroes.

These days the railroad is what stitches the country together—actually, that's always been true.

We also made arrangements regarding several future projects to support Ukrainian Railways and their passengers.

And we made arrangements about changing the names of regional railroads that are of Russian or Soviet origin after we win. And the tracks are numbered starting with Moscow—that will have to go. Let's start counting from Kyiv. Ukrainian Railways should be Ukrainian-centric.

Thanks for your work, my friends. :)

May 4, 7:54 p.m.

Over the past few weeks of war, old acquaintances have been calling from time to time. They say something like, "I'm fighting outside Kharkiv. We should get together." These meetings always surprise and invigorate me. On one hand, they're now so different: with bullet-proof vests, with weapons, with a different look in their eyes. On the other, the people are who they've always been; they haven't changed.

The people of Kharkiv who have been defending their city for over two months have so many heart-wrenching stories, stories that are often sad or often worthy of a bout of boisterous laughter. I remember one time I was walking with a guy from Rohan, heading back to the city from his post.

"Let's stop by my place," he requests. "I want to see if my house is still standing."

We swing by his neighborhood, and the ground is full

of craters, several apartment buildings burnt out, but there are these old guys sitting on a bench, just soaking up the evening sun. They offer a cordial greeting. The house is still standing, life goes on.

And today, I was so glad to see my pal Vasyl. Before the war, he would take spectacular pictures of Kharkiv in the evening time. He called, drove over, gave us a calendar with his artwork, and then headed back to his post, holding on to the firm conviction that after we win, the city will be no less beautiful than in his prewar photographs.

Rest up, my friends. Tomorrow, we'll wake up one day closer to our victory.

May 5, 1:08 p.m.

We met with the leadership of the Patrol Police of Ukraine the other day in Kharkiv (that was when Ivan and Andriy came to the city—I spoke about them like they were apostles). :) They're young officers who are now in charge of some very important things. Before the war, I would bump into most of them at festivals or pubs. My kind of folks, you know what they're about, not cut from the same cloth as the pre-Maidan cops. I'd really like for our government institutions to stay this way after we win: open, accessible, and free of that lingering Soviet taint. I realize that, as those who are trying to stay neutral in a time of war are so fond of saying, "things aren't so straightforward," and I don't have any illusions regarding the formation of a truly Ukrainian-centric state. It will be a challenging and lengthy process, but when you talk with these boys and girls, you want to believe in them. :)

One more thing. I told the head of the Patrol Police about getting slapped with a speeding ticket in Dnipro—we were driving Kharkiv-style . . . and we've gotten used to streets with no traffic lights. :)

He was a bit flustered, but actually we appreciate that the police have principles and are not biased. We were in the wrong, so it's all good. :) The police and the people are together. Sorry to get sentimental. :) Greetings to you all from Kharkiv.

May 6, 12:37 p.m.

We delivered two carloads of equipment to our friends from the 229th Battalion of the Territorial Defense Forces: a generator, tablet, laptop, shovels–construction staples–nails, two enormous rolls of insulation, walkie-talkies, backpacks, and food. The boys have their work cut out for them, so they have to be well equipped and well protected.

Talked a little about emotional intelligence and the fighters' morale with the officers. The commanders told us that young, inexperienced fighters often push forward when they ought to hold back. Those with experience know how to wait. They also said that the fighters were still fired up, despite the fatigue that had been building for the past few weeks.

The commander of the battalion mentioned that he'd accompanied German journalists around North Saltivka during the first days of the war and they'd come under Grad rocket fire. "Ever since then," he said, "I haven't been a huge fan of journalists or volunteers on the front lines." He did thank the volunteers, though, and he fired everyone up with his positive energy. :)

It's sunny and summery in Kharkiv, poplar fuzz flying, dandelions blazing yellow. The streets are a little dusty. Municipal workers drag cinder blocks where they need to go. :) Wind and springtime in the city. Ukrainian flags flutter above the city.

May 6, 5:23 p.m.

We went to one of Kharkiv's factories the other day. Since the start of the war, roughly four hundred people—employees, their families, people from the neighborhood and the region at large—have been hiding in its bomb shelters. The residents had organized themselves right away, divvied up their daily tasks, and set up a school for the kids. A Russian tank rolled by the factory one day, but our forces quickly fended it off.

These days, things are calm. There are about seventy people still living in the bomb shelter, mostly those who have lost their homes.

We brought them some food. They gave us a tour, showed us their setup. A mother was sitting in one of the rooms breastfeeding her baby. They were discharged from the maternity hospital on February 23, so the child has never known anything outside this basement. Their father is a firefighter. A girl named Dasha is reading something in the room they use as a school. Her teacher, Karolina, is keeping a close eye on the scene—though she's still of school age herself. :)

In the kitchen, the women say that they now have a Bandera salad and a Victory borscht on the menu.

The employees are *adamant* about speaking only Ukrainian. :) Sometimes they slip into Russian, but then they immediately switch back into Ukrainian.

We had a small reading. We agreed that we would hold a big concert after we won.

These are touching, piercing, warming voices, these are Kharkiv today. :)

May 6, 8:13 p.m.

Day 72 of the war.

Kharkiv's children sing "Red Viburnum." In Andriy Khlyvnyuk's expressive arrangement. :) These kids will sing completely different songs because they learned the lyrics under fire.

Have a quiet evening, dear brothers and sisters. Tomorrow, we'll wake up one day closer to our victory.

May 7, 1:13 p.m.

The Munich Biennale begins today. *The Songs of Exile and No Return* will open the festival. It's my libretto, and the wonderful Austrian composer Bernhard Gander wrote the music to it. I didn't fly in for the premiere, obviously, but I really hope people will see and hear the opera. We did this piece specifically for the biennale. I wrote the lyrics a year and a half ago. It ended up being a story about two men whom a country was trying to deport in wartime. One of the men fought for the country, while the other guy was a common criminal. There are a lot of refugees, migrants, bought-and-paid-for European politicians, and less-than-sincere burghers in the libretto. I wrote it without trying to make any predictions or projections, of course. It's just what I came up with. If you happen to be in Munich, enjoy the show. Thanks a lot to the organizers—that was some interesting and creative work. Wish us a nice premiere, I guess . . .

May 8, 12:22 a.m.

Well, we continue to prepare for Kharkiv's first wartime rock festival. After lengthy and exhausting negotiations, we recently reached an agreement—Serhiy Vasylyuk from Tin Sontsia and Number 482 with their frontman Vitaliy Kyrychenko will perform at the festival.

Rock and roll begins in eastern Ukraine. :)

May 8, 6:23 p.m.

If we're going to remember everyone who has fought Nazism, then we ought to listen to Mykola Bazhan's prophetic words: "Ukraine will never, ever be a slave to fascist butchers." Or ruscist butchers.

[. . .]

May 10, 12:59 p.m.

Kids from Ternopil sent a drawing to the defenders of Kharkiv.

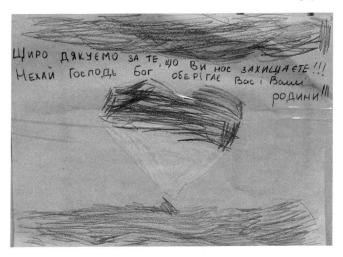

The heading reads, "I'm genuinely grateful that you're protecting us!!! May the Lord God look after you and your families!!!"

It's been cold in the city. The sky is stuffed with clouds. The early spring greenery is thick, striking.

We met with a unit commander. He showed us a video of a POW from the Donetsk People's Republic. He was scared, claiming that he'd just been shipped out and told to stand at a checkpoint. Our unit was deployed to the front; some are in combat and some supporting them—the boys have gotten to work. It's nice to see that everything we collected, bought, and delivered has been put to good use.

The city is quiet, but there are more and more pedestrians, more and more cars. Military vehicles are being hauled around, a Russian Nona, clearly captured by our forces, rolls down the street. The city council has announced that street names will be changed. In other words, "Moskovskiy Prospekt" will most likely be no more. :) It isn't huge, but I'll take it.

We ordered a bunch of cars. Now we're waiting for them to come in. We're waiting for other things we purchased to come in, too. Ukrainian forces should be well armed and surrounded with care. :) The sky is pure and blue behind the clouds. Ukrainian flags flutter above the city.

May 10, 3:20 p.m.

We just went to Skovorodynivka, dropped off two carloads of food for the locals, and visited our friends at the bombed-out Skovoroda Museum.

Looking at the burned remains of the building is painful. And trying to process all this is painful. Because there's simply no logic to bombing a museum. The thing is, though, you can't really trace the logic behind the Russians' actions in general. What you can trace is unhinged, shoreless, boundless evil, which we must defeat if we are to keep on living, loving, and doing what we hold dear.

May 10, 9:40 p.m.

Today, the director of the Museum of Childhood, Mr. Valeriy, and I went to visit the kids who have been staying at a factory in town since the beginning of all this. We read some poems and brought them a telescope so they could check out the moon. :)

The children are amazing, so happy, all smiles and high spirits. They thanked us for the candy we brought, contemplated the evening Kharkiv sky, and read their own poems. Even the factory director recited a poem he'd written as a kid. :) Originally from Donetsk, he moved to Kharkiv in 2014. But the war caught up to him here, too. :(

Our children shouldn't have to live through bombardments and air-raid warnings. And the sky above them
ought to be peaceful. Rocket-free. With a moon that
waxes slowly and beautifully, at the very least. Rest up,
my friends. Tomorrow, we'll wake up one day closer to
our victory :)

May 11, 8:46 a.m.

My grandpa smoked Cosmos cigarettes. I distinctly
associate them with him—and with my Soviet childhood,
which was subjectively sublime but objectively shaped
by a constant lack of necessary, yet basic, items, when
Cosmos cigarettes were a sign you were well off.

Our servicemen gave me this pack as a present. They
found it in a captured Russian tank outside of Kharkiv.
A "hello" of sorts from the Soviet past. After all, everything that Russia has been producing, articulating, and
demonstrating is a musty draft from the Soviet Union,
the corpse choked vent of the past. It's a lost, doomed
civilization that simply can't leave itself or others alone.

Well, and the warning label about how smoking kills
is quite apt, too. I'd add that smoking on someone else's
land, where nobody has invited you, kills. Greetings
from Ukrainian Kharkiv, dear brothers and sisters.

"Cosmos. Smoking Kills."

May 11, 5:58 p.m.

The city has warmed up. Moreover, it hasn't been bombarded for two days, which gives rise to the illusion of peacetime normalcy. Cars line up at the edge of the city—people are returning home to Kharkiv. Everyone misses their homes. Everyone misses their city.

Nevertheless, it's obvious that this is a shaky and rather dangerous illusion. Any corner of the city could still come under fire, we're still vulnerable, and the war is far from over. It simply has shifted, as it did eight years ago, to the east, to someplace in the Donbas. And you just don't want to think about the shelling in Ruska Lozova and Zolochiv, about another possible attack on the city, about any sort of danger.

Instead, I'd like to capture this day, if only for a single moment: the sharp, brisk wind whipping through the incinerated insides of the Kharkiv government building, the drowsy, half-empty train station, the Ivano-Frankivsk express packed with people returning home, the tears of pain and love, the empty dusty streets, the tape on servicemen's sleeves, and the steel in their eyes.

The city is coming back to life, rallying. Ukrainian flags flutter above the city.

May 12, 12:28 p.m.

We went to see our boys and girls outside the city, in a recently liberated village. A unit we've been actively loading up with necessary supplies for the past month is posted there. For them, this has been their baptism by fire, which they, I must say, have endured successfully and efficiently.

The village is quiet, empty, badly battered. There are hardly any undamaged buildings, and you can see a lot of burnt-out vehicles, civilian and military alike.

The servicemen said that they came under heavy bombardment when they got there. They talked about the strange feeling you have when you step into a house one day and it's gone the next day. They mentioned that they went into the local leader's house and found a Russian flag there. The Russians bombed that house the next day.

Our forces are pushing forward, liberating towns and villages, and they aren't planning on stopping. :) It was interesting to watch the commanders at work—they're loud, always shouting themselves hoarse, but always maintaining good order. We have the best army: Ukrainian, of the people, our own. Greetings to you all from Ukrainian Kharkiv.

May 13, 8:35 p.m.

The Russians bombed the house of culture in Derhachi. The Dogs and I loved that place. We rehearsed there several times, recorded "Trees" and "Cocaine" there, performed on the steps outside the building once, and tried to organize a big concert for the town's residents.

More senseless destruction. The Russian aggressors are destroying everything in their path. Schools, libraries, churches, houses of culture. They're simply bothered by everything that's part of our lives. They're destroying everything that's important and meaningful to us, while brazenly and cynically claiming to pursue some strategic aims.

Make no mistake, we'll have a concert in Derhachi. After we win. Rest up, my friends. Summer is under way. We all have a lot of work to do. And this work will deliver results, for all of us, for our country. Tomorrow, we'll wake up one day closer to our victory.

May 14, 8:19 a.m.

For the past few weeks, I've been posting pictures of equipment, uniforms, vehicles, and other important things that we've ordered, bought, collected, and obtained for one of Kharkiv's new units, my friends. During this time, we've actually managed to send them an ambulance, several pickups, dozens of bulletproof vests, helmets, a load of high-quality military boots, uniforms, jackets, gloves, goggles, and sleeping bags–sleeping pads–mattresses, as well as drones, thermal imagers, night-vision devices, walkie-talkies, and generators.

I didn't write about the unit itself, though. It was just being formed, so that would have been a little premature. Well, it's been a little over a week since the fighters took up their positions north of Kharkiv and went through their baptism by fire (there are a lot of seasoned fighters who have some serious military experience under their belts, though), captured their first POWs—and their first artillery piece. :) Yet another solid unit that is expanding and getting more weapons with each passing day has come to the defense of Kharkiv. This new formation is called *Khartiya,* "The Charter."

Remember that name. :) It's a volunteer community unit—in other words, these are people from Kharkiv who have come together to defend their city. And they're pretty good at it.

A lot of people I know are fighting for this unit. Basically, my friends and I were standing right there at the inception and formation of Khartiya—I even came up with the name for them. :) So to a great extent, this is our unit, and we continue to provide them with whatever they need—but not without your help, naturally.

We ordered a bunch of walkie-talkies, several vehicles, and uniforms (the number of fighters continues to grow) and are waiting for them to be delivered. Well, I'll keep reporting on Khartiya's activities. The boys have plenty of work to do. They have plenty of ardor, too, though.

Thank you all for your support and assistance. Everything will be all right, everything will be Ukraine. Together to victory!

May 15, 2:01 p.m.

Here's another post about birthday boys. :)

Today is the birthday of a longtime friend of mine, the brilliant—I'm not afraid to use that word—actor Misha Ozerov. On the first day of the Russian invasion, Misha called me and said I could hide out in their theater's bomb shelter. Things didn't pan out with the bomb shelter, but Misha and I bumped into each other on the street about a week later, and it turned out that he and his actor friends were doing a lot of volunteer work, assisting civilians, and delivering humanitarian aid—in other words, they were working conscientiously and systematically. So we started working together. :)

Over the past two months, we've driven hundreds of kilometers around the city and region in Misha's car (actually, I got it for him, but whatever—let's call it a birthday present), gone to a few hair-raising places, and met a boatload of fantastic people.

So I'd like to take this opportunity to wish Misha a happy birthday, joy, goodness, and victory for us all. :) Buddy, you're an awesome guy with a pure soul, a big heart, and true Ukrainian talent. Health and happiness to you. And don't go blowing through any traffic lights. :)

P.S. Misha asked me to post a rough list of everything we have fundraised for and say that for him, the best gift would be to support our volunteer efforts. [. . .]

And here's what we have collected, bought, "commandeered," handed over to, and spread among our servicemen, give or take:

6 chainsaws

30 regular shovels

10 sapper shovels

8 generators

150 pairs of shoes for our troops, plus 50 pairs of
    combat boots

100 bulletproof vests

50 load-bearing vests

12 thermal imagers

3 drones

6 cars

62 helmets

10 laptops

10 tablets

3 TVs

6 electric kettles

5 microwaves

6 gas heaters

7 flashlights

1 repaired minibus

14 tires

2 washers

2 cellphones

military clothes for 100 persons

1,125 pairs of socks

130 pairs of underwear

165 T-shirts for servicemen

4 walkie-talkies

60 pairs of gloves (48,000 hryvnias)

50 jackets (70,000 hryvnias)

1 pistol holster

90 military jackets

1 sniper scope

4 submachine-gun cases

4 more washers

100 sleeping pads

150 sleeping bags

10 binoculars

2 monoculars

19 pairs of military gloves

In addition to all that, a facility run by actors has been providing meals for several hundred people in Kharkiv on a daily basis for the past several weeks. I love and respect him—that's all I have to say. :)

May 16, 8:49 a.m.

I received a helmet and bulletproof vest from our unit and was told not to come out to their position without them. Hamlet, the artist, signed them, too. So I have two pieces of artwork now. After the war, I'll sell them for a lot of money and rebuild a school. Greetings to you all from Ukrainian Kharkiv.

May 16, 8:19 p.m.

The city switches to a peacetime schedule so quickly. And that's a good thing. :) Yet it's important to remember that the war is far from over, and that the Kharkiv Region is getting walloped as cruelly as the city itself recently was. :(

Public transportation is running in the city again. And what a surprise it is to see buses with passengers inside and people waiting at the stops. :)

More and more coffee shops are opening back up. Folks sit there smoking hookahs leisurely. The coffee shops that opened first, several weeks ago, are crammed with foreign journalists. :) They're looking for ways to get to active combat zones, since things have been more or less calm in the city, thanks to the Armed Forces of Ukraine. An old man sits outside the Shevchenko Theatre and plays a barrel organ. :)

I walk into a pet shop that also houses a beer shop— Altbier heroically brews delicious beer. :) There aren't any customers, so the two clerks, as per a long-standing Ukrainian custom, are arguing. It took me a bit to figure out what the matter was.

"*Raklo* is a word only used in Kharkiv," one of them said.

"Nah," the other woman objected. "It's used all over Ukraine."

"Nah," the first woman insisted, "it came from Kharkiv, but now Ukrainians everywhere use it to mean 'swindler.'"

In other words, questions of identity have come to the surface. It's a little chilly and windy in the city. Ukrainian flags flutter above the city (by the way, they're all over the place—on apartment complexes, above administrative buildings, on cars—and thank God). :)

May 18, 10:26 a.m.

Yesterday, we held an event at the Museum of Childhood for kids who have been staying in the metro in Saltivka for over two months. Despite everything, the kids are cheerful, albeit somewhat skeptical. They crack jokes, support each other, and take an interest in everything. They're waiting for new accommodations. Most of them no longer have homes.

It was strange to watch them sitting among old Soviet toy guns and real Trypillia pottery. I'd really like there to be less Soviet junk in their lives and more real Ukraine. We read some poems, gave them some treats, and agreed to meet after we win. :)

Greetings to you all from Ukrainian Kharkiv. :)

May 19, 8:52 a.m.

I went to North Saltivka. My friends asked me to see if their apartment building was still standing. It was, and the door was closed, but the buildings nearby were terribly battered. These were the buildings that face the road that runs around the city. I remember coming here on Day 2 of the war. Our servicemen had already managed to take out the first Russian columns. The buildings were still intact. We even managed to record an interview between bouts of shelling. Now the whole neighborhood has been obliterated. The building next to my friends', where I lived for several years, is black and charred.

The locals clear the rubble bit by bit, try to settle back in, salvage what's left of their things, and get their cars out. Somebody talks about a shell stuck in a couch, somebody else jokes about looters.

It's warm and sunny. There are rumbling sounds coming from out by Tsyrkuny.

May 19, 10:17 a.m.

We just did a full-fledged studio recording. For some reason, this war's got me singing about kids more than anything. Maybe because they're the ones who need to be protected the most during all of this. Take care of each other, dear brothers and sisters.

May 19, 6:42 p.m.

Went to the area outside of Barvinkiv, where their library burned down. Some locals asked us to bring books for their new future library and for the servicemen to read in the meantime. I reached out to Oleksandr "Sasha" Krasovytskiy, who has donated a ton of books from Folio Publishers to libraries in eastern Ukraine over the course of the past eight years. This time around, Sasha donated two thousand titles—mostly fiction and history books. My hat is off to him. :) The books are where they're supposed to be, and we'll go open the library after we win. :)

I'm fully aware that many feel this isn't the time for cultural initiatives and projects, but for me, someone who has spent the past few years filling dozens of libraries with new titles, I simply want to protect, in a literal, physical sense, our cultural sites that are being destroyed by the "second strongest army in the world," which is actually very clumsy. Human life is the most valuable thing, of course. But what's the meaning of this life without museums, theaters, libraries, and bookstores? Please excuse my sentimentality. :)

May 19, 9:57 p.m.

These days, it's green and windy outside the city. Some utterly unreal clouds have sprawled across Sloboda Ukraine.

You may fall under the fleeting illusion that everything is quiet and peaceful. Until you run into yet another checkpoint. Or yet another monument to soldiers who served in World War II. These monuments seem so strange amid today's reality.

Vehicles race across fields, stirring up dust. Old ladies sit on benches in their villages and soak up the sun. As you get closer to Barvinkiv, the villages grow tense. Hardly anyone is outside. We gave two carloads of meds and food to some local activists. The evening sky is bloody. It's as if a purple ray was bursting out of the earth.

It's almost summertime. We all need lots of energy and perseverance. So rest up, my friends. Tomorrow, we'll wake up one day closer to our victory.

May 20, 3:08 p.m.

Kharkiv was bombarded again last night. You could even hear it in the city center. The windows were ringing. Things had quieted down by the morning, though. The city is coming back to life.

A bookstore opened back up. :) That's a little thing, but still worth celebrating. There are a lot of amazing people who miss each other.

You can immediately pick out newcomers—they talk about apartments, try to figure out what's open and what's not. They're sentimental, easily moved.

Foreign journalists persistently continue asking about our attitude toward Pushkin. :)

As you walk around the city, you might bump into a bunch of people from Kyiv. :) Servicemen bring good news from the front lines. :)

It's summertime in the city. Ukrainian flags flutter above the city. :)

May 21, 9:38 a.m.

Thick smoke hovered over the city—something has been smoldering since this morning.

Smells like somebody's burning books. This lull, which stirred and invigorated us, wound up being just that—a lull. Yesterday, smoke hovered over various neighborhoods in the city. Off toward Derhachi, a streak of incoming fire hung in the air awhile. It was like a comet had fallen.

Our enemies have reminded us that they're here, that this isn't over, that it's too early to ease up. We haven't forgotten that, though.

Greetings to you all from Ukrainian Kharkiv.

May 21, 1:07 p.m.

Fourteen-year-old Alisa made this drawing in one of Kharkiv's basements. I've had occasion to see many different shelters in these nearly three months of war. And many different children. Seeing children in bomb shelters or the metro is particularly painful, of course. I do have to say, though, that they come out of those basements, and when they do, they're completely different people, who know the lyrics to our anthem and "Red Viburnum." From here on out, I would like them to use the metro strictly as passengers, though.

Our children understand everything perfectly well—the whole world is on our side. There's nothing to add. I can merely join them—Glory to Ukraine. :)

The words read, "Glory to Ukraine / The whole world is on our side!"

The silence outside, heavy and somehow harsh, woke me up. Then a siren sounded, and I fell right back to sleep.

I was running around town yesterday. It looks so strange: cars at traffic lights, more young people out and about, yet there are checkpoints and regular sirens. The city hasn't fully processed what has happened to it these past three months. Moreover, so many things (and so many scary things) have taken place that what we need is not time but a sense of conclusion.

It's hard to talk about rebuilding and renaming streets if those streets are still being shelled. This talk about the future after our victory is rather abstract, of course, just hovering in the air, but it's therapeutic, too. We aren't afraid of talking about time and perseverance, no matter where that time is headed.

It's understandable that we want to cling to life outside the war or that we react optimistically or with surprise to every store that reopens or tram that starts running again—so fast it feels like they're gonna fly off the tracks, like usual. :)

Yet you look out the window, it's morning, and there's an explosion very close by. The war goes on, the city wakes up, and Ukrainian flags flutter above the city.

May 24, 4:07 p.m.

This train is long, ramshackle. The cars are all different. Some of them are brand-new, others are all shabby. They've clearly been strung together from different trains. The numbers of the cars were printed on Xerox paper. Apparently, these cars are used on lots of different routes, so the numbers change constantly.

The train steals slowly up to the platform, as if it's peering out to see how safe things are here in eastern Ukraine. The train attendants are a little worn out, yet happy. They made it, after all. Tape crisscrosses the windows.

On the platform are serious-looking, taciturn servicemen holding flowers and toys—they're greeting their family members. They're somewhat anxious, somewhat bewildered.

The passengers cheerfully step out onto the platform. Some of them can't hold back their tears—they've returned home. Once again, there's a lot of movement and voices in the city. The city returns to life, comes to its senses. There's so much energy and love in it now, and Ukrainian flags flutter overhead.

May 24, 6:07 p.m.

If I'm being totally honest, the Dogs and I tried to write something about the war back in March. What we came up with was overblown, patriotic, and not all that deep. Reality proved more potent than our notions about it and our ability to articulate them. Then I met two boys in the Kharkiv metro. I've already written about them here. They helped the grown-ups, maintained order, and organized activities for the "munchkins"—in short, they're all grown up already. :) Well, this song was written after that.

Throughout these three months of war (THREE MONTHS OF WAR), I've had the chance to see a lot of Kharkiv kids: getting them out of the city, singing for them in the metro, or bringing them food in bomb shelters. All kinds of kids: taciturn and frightened, cheerful and confident, some with a childish brashness about them, others constantly stressed. But they're all still our kids, from Kharkiv. I really want them to keep living in this strange, sublime city (or to return to it if their elders have taken them away). I really want them to love this city. To feel they can speak openly. To have that Kharkiv brashness and not to be afraid of the world adults have left them.

[. . .]

May 25, 8:36 a.m.

Good morning to you all from Ukrainian Kharkiv.

We've entered month four of the war, my friends. Much has changed during this time—from the situation on the front lines to our attitudes and emotions. These three months have been pretty tough on Kharkiv—the city was simply being demolished; constant mass shelling engulfed entire neighborhoods. Kharkiv withstood all that, though. First and foremost, thanks to our servicemen, who were able to restrain the occupiers and repel them from the outskirts of Kharkiv. As well, thanks to everyone who has been supporting our armed forces all these months and efficiently providing them with all the supplies they need.

The city has been relatively calm and quiet lately. Despite the fact that the Russians continue shelling different neighborhoods here and there, the city is returning to a semblance of normalcy; the people of Kharkiv are returning to their homes.

Obviously, our servicemen are the ones making this peaceful existence possible. The war is far from over. Fighting continues right next to the city. Part of the Kharkiv Region is occupied. It's too early to ease up—still a lot of work and challenges ahead of us. What matters most, though, is that our victory is ahead of us too, and we can bring it a little closer by continuing to support our army, one way or another.

What am I trying to say? I think that those reading this page have been involved since the first day of Russia's full-scale invasion and have been helping Ukraine however they can. So I hope I'm talking to people who are all on the same wavelength. I'd like to reach out, first and foremost, to those Ukrainians who have been living abroad for a while now, who haven't lost their jobs due to the Russian attack, who were not forced to leave, look for a new place to live and settle in during these past three months. We have been shifting our focus toward assisting the army. Our servicemen still need a lot of things: cars, drones, rangefinders, thermal imagers, optical imaging systems, etc. These things are needed in large quantities as there's a lot of wear and tear involved (I'm mostly referring to cars and drones). The army would be struggling much more without our support. In this situation, we have to hold out and persevere by letting our servicemen lean on us. We simply cannot afford to lose. We have to crush our enemy and liberate our territory.

During the past week, our team has ordered and paid for, and is now expecting, several cars, drones, and a great deal of military equipment, which we'll transfer to our servicemen. We also have a lot of orders from other units. We appreciate any help. We'll keep working, working toward our victory.

Glory to Ukraine!

May 25, 8:58 p.m.

Today, on Philology Day, Stanislav Borysovych Stasevsky, distinguished linguist and head of the Ukrainian
Language and Literature Department at Skovoroda
Kharkiv National Pedagogical University for many years,
passed away. My first academic mentor. I remember going to my college interview in the summer of '91: Professor Stasevsky was part of the admissions committee,
and after meeting him, we all—everyone who was getting interviewed, I mean—realized that we'd made the
right choice. He elicited trust and respect. I remember
that we all really did love him; nobody fawned over him,
we just loved him the way only students can. He was
disciplined, yet open, strict at times, yet never brusque.
It was remarkable how he managed to combine these
traits. He followed prescribed procedures and demands,
but he did it with sincerity and humanity.

The thing is, we language majors at Skovoroda University in the early nineties got really lucky with our professors: studying under Leonid Ushkalov or Kim Kho-
mych Balabukha was a real joy. They were so filled with
love for literature and the written word that you always
felt as if you belonged when you were alongside them.
This feeling of being with my own people, people united
by the word, is perhaps the warmest and most radiant of
my college memories.

These people—professors, experts, specialists in their fields—have really done so much over the past thirty years by nurturing several generations of linguists and literary scholars. One can only imagine just how many children have been nurtured at Kharkiv Pedagogical (there probably are official statistics on this, but I'm a language major, so I phrased it more poetically). :)

I really love these people, I really appreciate my professors, and I'm terribly disheartened by Professor Stasevsky's passing. Nevertheless, it's nice to remember a person whom I loved and sincerely respected. Enduring love and respect are very valuable and truly invigorating.

Rest in peace, Professor!

May 26, 4:14 p.m.

Kharkiv is being brutally shelled once again. There are casualties once again. The tenuous and illusory calm that has persisted, more or less, to a certain extent, over the past few days, has been interrupted, as expected, by new explosions.

Once again, there's the constant feeling that we all had during the first two months—that there's no rhyme or reason to anything, that you aren't able to influence anything. When you drive through an intersection and then find out on the news that it was shelled ten minutes later.

I feel bad for people who cling to their peacetime existence and whose peacetime existence slides through their fingers like a predatory fish.

I don't even know who has it rougher—those who have recently returned to our quiet, sunny city and now have to experience the horrors of shelling or those people who stayed down in the metro for two months, then eventually agreed to come out so the metro could start running again, and found themselves, once again, in a situation akin to late February–early March.

The war is somewhere near all the time. It loves reminding everyone of its presence.

Even the weather has taken a turn for the worse. It's raining in Kharkiv. Ukrainian flags still flutter overhead, though.

May 29, 5:25 p.m.

Kharkiv is still being bombarded. They won't let the city wholly return to its calm existence. Clearly, the city will face numerous challenges, and it won't be anything like it was before for some time. Even if you start dreaming about life in peacetime, it isn't all that clear what will become of those who have left or who will return.

What will become of the students—the foreign students, in particular. What will become of the city's economy. Simply put, we have our work cut out for us. And I'd really like to get started right away. I'd really like to refurbish, repair, and rebuild everything. I'd really like to see Kharkiv strong and confident. I should also mention that we received an amazing drone from Oleh Kadanov's friends yesterday, and we've already given it to our unit. We also got a whole carload of meds and handed those over to two units. We procured a ton of entrenching tools (shovels, nails, construction staples, etc.) for our boys in Zolochiv and Mala Rohana. Simply put, we're hard at work, thanks to your support.

Clouds have been hovering above the city since morning, and it's been raining all day. Ukrainian flags flutter above the city.

May 29, 9:25 p.m.

I keep catching myself thinking that Kharkiv's art scene has been on hold since February 24. It has stopped sharply, like in a game of freeze tag. It's a very strange feeling, a bitter one, but it still leaves hope that this feeling will unfreeze soon.

For instance, we planned to put on the premiere of Brecht's *Mother Courage* in my translation at a puppet theater in late February (it's remarkable just how different Brecht's story about the Thirty Years' War and people trying to survive the meat grinder of the front lines sounds these days), and Stepan Pasichnyk was supposed to produce *Maklena Grasa* at the Shevchenko Theatre (we met right there on the stage, where the set hadn't even been taken down; seeing art augment reality, become interchangeable with it, grow adjoined to it is a keenly heart-wrenching feeling). Oleh Kalashnyk's fantastically powerful and chilling exhibition, which features toy soldiers from Soviet children's play sets, opened on February 22 at YermilovCentre. There were also dozens of planned presentations, concert posters, creative endeavors, and ambitious art projects.

The city's cultural scene awaits its hour, and I have to say that without the voice of art and culture Kharkiv feels quiet—strangely so.

Clearly, everything will come back, everything will start working again—that's how important this artistic element is to our city. For now, though, we have to relish every underground concert, every reopened bookstore, and every theater rehearsal.

All of this is within reach. Even if, for now, the city is quiet and the concert halls are empty. Everything will be all right.

Rest up, dear brothers and sisters—tomorrow, we'll wake up one day closer to our victory.

[. . .]

May 30, 10:03 p.m.

Over the past few weeks, it's been nice to write about "things returning to normal" (this is a terrible phrase that doesn't actually explain what's going on at all or put anyone at ease): stores or restaurants in the city opening up again, traffic lights working again, people returning to their homes. Now, though, I can't get myself to write about all that. Because this sense of normalcy is notional, at best, and extremely dangerous. Now expensive cars line the perimeter of a city square again, and teenagers do tricks on their terrible freestyle bikes again, yet the constant shelling—both in the city proper and outside town—make this illusion of normalcy in the warm, sunny city a mere melancholy specter. These days, life in Kharkiv is akin to living in a communal apartment with a bunch of drunks. And if your neighbors aren't smashing dishes in the kitchen, that simply means that they haven't woken up yet after the previous day's festivities. If we aren't getting hit, that means that our drunk neighbors are simply bringing in more weapons. This isn't exactly the most pleasant feeling, but what can you do? Nobody is planning on moving out. Nobody is going to kowtow to those drunks—they don't deserve it.

In the evenings, Kharkiv is so quiet and empty. Summer—even if it's a bit chilly, not exactly a scorcher—has already inundated the streets. The sky above the city is vast and mysterious. Evenings already have a summery depth and endlessness to them.

Rest up, dear brothers and sisters. Tomorrow, we'll wake up one day closer to our victory.

May 31, 9:11 a.m.

Good morning to you all from Kharkiv.

I'd like to say something, my friends. You've been helping out and fundraising all these years (I mean since the war started in 2014, not since February 24). I'm used to being a bank account—or a safe deposit box of sorts :)—where funds are transferred and then they go toward assisting Ukrainians, civilians and servicemen alike. I always genuinely appreciate that. Unfortunately, I simply don't have time to thank everyone personally. :(Sometimes this assistance is so unexpected and touching. Actually, though, every transfer—from ten dollars to a thousand euros—is touching and worthy of appreciation, since it can save someone's life.

Yet truly unexpected things happen sometimes. Like the Polish author Kazimierz Orłoś donating part of his literary prize to support Kharkiv. This is an important and very kind gesture that speaks to Poland's support of Ukraine. Tough times like these reveal who's really a good neighbor or who will watch your barn burn down. :)

Thank you all for supporting our city, my friends. Let there always be peaceful skies above it. :)

Here's a little more about Kazimierz and the prize: "Writer Kazimierz Orłoś has donated part of his honorarium from the Marek Nowakowski Literary Award, granted by the National Library of Poland in Warsaw, to support Kharkiv. He received this prize for his ongoing contribution to the literary community throughout a career that has already lasted for 60 years. Mr. Orłoś's daughter Joanna heads the Izabela Cultural Center that will be organizing Izabela's Meetings with a Book on June 10–12, which will have a Ukrainian program, screen *Slovo House,* and hold a charity fundraiser for Kharkiv, sponsored by Hnat Khotkevych Palace of Culture" (another famous resident of Kharkiv, actually).

June 1, 9:24 a.m.

I'm joining New York Literary Festival's #fightthemwithpoetry fundraiser for the Armed Forces of Ukraine! We had a reading in New York—the recently renamed town in Ukraine, I mean—just last year. And we'll be back! Put your trust in the Armed Forces of Ukraine!

For a whole month, they stood by this river.
For a whole month, this river stood still, so close.
No fire could be lit, smokers stayed silent.
And on this side, soldiers stood.
And on that side, too, soldiers stood.

A black river,

onward flows a black river.

Being with it for so long is tough.

It's so deep, so slimy in August.

What will it be like when it flows into the Sea of

    Azov?

Hearts pumping audibly in the dark,

nobody knew how it'd all end.

And the current carried a corpse down from the

    north,

in no hurry, like all corpses.

Like it'd been brought by lasting misfortune,

pulled in different directions.

Water pooled in its punctured lungs—

the sweet black water of a river set in the steppe,

Get out of here, dead man, go beyond the banks,

take your death and your fear with you,

we, the living, lack vigor here,

so what's a dead man to do on these banks?

Take your death with you, take it,

take it far away from this river,

take it out of the dark current,

take your dead fists out of here.

The current cut the warm ore.

The crescent glimmered in the fox's eyes.

And there he lay, arms splayed, on the August

    water,

heavy as a cross on a man's shoulders.
And then he drifted down the riverbed some-
    where to the east,
drifted along the boundless bottom,
and the men on shore watched him go,
and cried for this corpse,
for yet another corpse.
The land of frightened fish and steppe birds.
The land of golden wheat and burnt grass—
one day, somebody will write the history of these
    banks,
the history of these channels and crossings.
Somebody will insert all the names,
the names of sharp acacias and green nettles.
The right bank—the moon bounces off it.
The left bank—no one retreats from it.

June 1, 12:29 p.m.

We're reopening the LF Music Club soon, my friends. Because what kind of city doesn't have a rock club? Kharkiv must ring out, loudly and convincingly, especially when they're trying to force us to stay silent and disappear. See you at our concerts!

June 1, 4:21 p.m.

We just wished kids from three communities—Babai, Khroly, and Rohan (the Kharkiv Region has some great names)—a happy International Children's Day. Zheka Turchynov and I sang, a local puppet theater put on a show, and Vivat Publishing House gave the kids some books. We brought the little munchkins some treats, too. In short, it was a real celebration. Thank you to Mykola Blahovestov and Natalia Pakhnina for organizing it.

The kids were wonderful. They enjoyed the songs and fairy tales. Now they've entered this uncertain, war-torn summer, wholly relying on their parents, teachers, and other adults. What will this summer be like for them? What about this fall?

Meanwhile, it's quiet on the outskirts of town: old ladies sit on benches and talk about family problems, quiet drunks scour the area, their shadows passing between prefab buildings, and a child cries on one of the top floors. Then the crying ceases—apparently, the little one has calmed down. Outgoing fire can be heard from the north. A Ukrainian helicopter flies toward the city. The city over the mountains is large and sunny. Ukrainian flags flutter above the city.

June 5, 11:15 a.m.

In the morning, the city is cloudy and completely quiet—all you can hear is the birds singing. There are puddles from the summer showers and front yards filled with flowers in the older sections of town. Fishermen stand above the riverbed—looks like they enjoy simply standing together, in silence.

Empty schoolyards have become overgrown.

More pedestrians are out and about in the early afternoon. They aren't really in a hurry, though—it's Sunday, and their movements are infused with languid tenderness. The bicyclists on the road are focused—they're running errands, clearly going somewhere, not just riding around town.

The shattered storefronts in the city center somehow immediately remind me of the tumultuous 1990s. This war is, to a great extent, an attempt to stop time, to slow it down. They're trying to impose a return to the past. It was a painful process, but we managed to escape it (rather successfully, I must say).

Amid all of this, Kharkiv is coming back to life, little by little, regaining its natural vigor and dynamism. Like someone doing exercises after they've broken their arm. They haven't lost the limb, thank God; it can be fixed. They're willing to put in the work, but all the time, aggravation, and wasted potential—now that's a real shame. The most important thing, though, is that they haven't lost their limbs, and they aren't afraid to put in the work.

The sun has come out. There's a summery translucence to things. Ukrainian flags flutter above the city.

June 5, 4:47 p.m.

My dear friend Andriy Lyubka and his Serbian colleague Vladimir Arsenijević sent two ambulances from the Medical Assistance Committee in Transcarpathia to the Kharkiv Region. One vehicle for the Derhachi Regional Hospital and the other for the hospital in Blyzniuky. Folks from Transcarpathia loaded up one vehicle with medical supplies for the Blyzniuky municipality, while Vladimir loaded the other one with diapers, children's food, and a ventilator for the Kharkiv Regional Children's Hospital. Simply put, this is exactly the kind of aid we need.

The first vehicle has already reached Derhachi. The other one will head out tomorrow. Considering the sheer number of supplies sent by folks in Transcarpathia, we agreed that we simply have to rename one of the streets in Derhachi Transcarpathian Street after we win.

I also have to mention our fearless doctors. They're the best: they have stayed put, kept working during all the bombardments, and kept believing in our victory. And I wish you all the same faith. :)

June 7, 4:23 p.m.

It's hot in Kharkiv. Every day, I get a call or a text from a friend, and they all say the same thing—"I'm back." Pushkinska Street is packed again.

I've bumped into a homeless man I've known awhile several times. Seems like he's been here this whole time—at the very least, I've seen him on Naukova and Pushkinska streets and around the square. These days, his hair's a little shorter; he walks by the front of a restaurant that has a sign that reads "We're Open Again" with that same pensive, detached air he's always had. Grass pokes through cobblestones in the city's squares and reminds everyone of time and its intractability.

The sky above Rohan is vast, slightly scorched, and meticulously filled with clouds. On one side, there's the bright, expansive streak of the sun. On the other, a faint, yet clearly delineated crescent. The clouds are scattered neatly. Basically, the sky looks like an old lady's well-manicured garden in Sloboda Ukraine.

In the areas where there are mostly single-family homes, you can't help but notice when people have left their houses and when they have stayed. When there's someone living there, the grass is neatly cut, the flower gardens are manicured, and the fences are painted white, even if they've been damaged by shrapnel.

The evening creeps up slowly. The evening is bountiful, unhurried. You can hear outgoing fire from the north. Ukrainian flags flutter above the city.

June 8, 2:19 p.m.

The city is weary from the sun: lazy, dusty, and still half-empty. It's as though half the city has gone to their dachas or the seaside, as in the good old days.

There are serious, respectable folks at a Georgian restaurant in town—men talking business and arguing over the phone. No nonsense. That's like the old days, too.

Teenagers rumble through the park on their skateboards; an old lady hobbles toward them, holding a bag of stuff in one hand and two little blue and yellow flags in the other. It's mostly elderly people on the benches in the square—some of them are talking on the phone, others reading something.

Friends discuss what areas got hit the day before when they see each other. It's like they're talking about the weather: where it rained, where a hailstorm damaged a cherry tree, where one missed.

This is a strange summer on the frontlines . . . Ukrainian flags flutter above the city.

June 10, 10:14 a.m.

Last year, on December 6, we had a concert in Severo-donetsk for Ukrainian Armed Forces Day. The boys and girls wore masks—at that time, Covid was our biggest problem. :) Some of those in attendance knew who we were, others had never heard of us. The brass was in attendance, so the rank-and-file soldiers didn't go too wild. Generally, concerts for troops in the field can get a little out of hand. :)

Then we hung out at the headquarters, listened to the soldiers' tall tales, alarming predictions, and words spoken with confidence by people for whom this war had been going on for eight years.

Now you look at this photograph like it's the echo of a different time, a different life. Now what will become of them? Now what will become of this hall? What will become of the city?

Clearly, everyone was ready for all this. Clearly, the people in this hall didn't wind up here by accident. Everyone realized that there was a war going on. Just like it's going on to this day. Nobody stepped aside, though. Because stepping aside on your own land isn't really an option.

Put your trust in the Armed Forces of Ukraine. Support the Armed Forces of Ukraine. Everything will be all right, everything will be Ukraine.

June 10, 2:28 p.m.

Greenery has flooded the outskirts of town. You can't feel the war at all out here. But then as we're driving down the road, someone says, "Remember this place got hit two days back? Right here, off to the left. They've already cleaned everything up, though."

Looking at the old checkpoints that were erected somewhat erratically, chaotically, around towns late in the winter is interesting. Now the war has crept northward; the men who stood behind mounds of old car tires with hunting rifles in February now have solid military experience. The war has slid out of winter into spring, and now it's drying up into a sweltering summer.

Typically, a merry bunch—drunks and beggars—lazily soaks up the sun in the square outside the train station, joined by security guards and pigeons, of course. There's a train arriving from Lviv: the anxious faces of those returning, the emotional faces of those greeting them. The crowd sprawls out into the square, taxi drivers swoop in and pick up their passengers and take them to scorching summer neighborhoods. Ukrainian flags flutter above the city.

June 11, 7:49 a.m.

I've often asked myself one question: Who exactly fought in the army of the Ukrainian People's Republic? I don't mean their social background or some sort of geographical breakdown. I mean the specifics of what motivated them. In memoirs or fiction (not from the Soviet period, of course—Heaven forbid), we are often presented with two distinct images. First were the well-educated idealists, but there was a catastrophic dearth of them, and then there were the more plentiful and uncouth types who were faced with the choice between warlords ruling local fiefdoms or true Ukrainian statehood and opted to go home and finish the harvest.

And what does this all mean for Ukraine's forces to-day? I realize that such comparisons are imprecise or flawed, but tracking, tracing the threads of people's paths, particular cases, and real-life stories that shape the design and backdrop of the Ukrainian forces is truly fascinating. Are there really historical parallels, or is this a different story altogether? The story of a people that assembled, clothed, and fed their forces all on their own. I have to say that the situation today is completely different from the confrontation that took place a hundred years ago—from the "army without a people" that was doomed to fail because it didn't have anything it could rely on during that disjointed in-between time.

The opposite is true for our boys and girls who have gone off to fight: their country really does stand behind them. They have a country they can rely on.

That's where the voices and stories I've heard over the past hundred-plus days come from.

Like the story of a volunteer who had fought in the Donbas and then returned home. He had sent all his loved ones to western Ukraine and showed up at the army recruiting office by lunchtime on February 24. Now he's the commander of a unit; he's been training the new recruits, sharing his experience, and waiting for when he'll be able to go pick up his family.

Or there's the story of a guy from Rohan who was drafted—whenever he returns to his hometown, he heads to his neighborhood to see what's what, says "hello" to all the old ladies sitting outside his building, listens to the local drunks' reports, and then heads back to his post with a sense of relief.

Or the story of a woman who used to teach Ukrainian but has now joined a battalion with her husband. They are stationed in a field outside the city: all of them are locals, all of them are from here, all of them have the city at their backs—not just any city, but a city where their homes and their futures are. I suspect we will all have countless accounts like these, boundless marveling at the vicissitudes of human life, and boundless surprise at the intersections of our upbringing, politics, and commitments. We are used to saying that history repeats itself. Sometimes it really does. Yet other times, you can adjust its routes to your own benefit. That's what's happening now.

Good morning, everyone.

June 11, 9:22 p.m.

It was Maria's last day of school: the last bell, as it's called here in Ukraine. The students, scattered across different cities and countries, were so glad to see each other on their screens.

I remember last September, the beginning of the school year, their hopes and aspirations: new school building, new teachers, everyone had finally switched to Ukrainian. This is what hurts so acutely now: destroyed schools, children forced to live in other cities, teachers out of work. Russia isn't just ruining our educational system, which is our future, it's bringing its narratives to our schools, the ones that are still standing, and wrecking everything we have been struggling to build for so long.

They've completely disregarded the fact that we do have agency, the fact that we're different; there's this heavy-handed, pervasive imposition of the way they do things, as if it's the only way. They can't do things differently; they're trained only to destroy and supplant.

One way or another, we have to protect our children from all that. So they can go to regular Ukrainian schools on September 1.

Rest up, my friends. The kids are off for the summer, but we have our work cut out for us. Tomorrow, we'll wake up one day closer to our victory.

June 12, 12:46 p.m.

I've thought about how many times I've had the chance to experience the city in completely different, surprising, and unexpected ways over the past few months, about how multi-layered it can be, how many secret hiding places and unexpected angles it has. It's as though you know everything about it (actually, you know far from everything, of course), yet it's still capable of changing its tone and telling you a heartfelt story that makes you fall in love in an absolutely new way.

It's like your father's junk drawer—you know every item in it down to the last paper, old watch, or broken cufflink, but then you open it one day and something unexpected catches your eye, something nobody needs at all—which doesn't make it any less valuable. I remember Slava Vakarchuk and I went to see the mayor during the first few weeks of the siege. We did some talking and listening. After that, he suggested we take a walk over to the nearby metro station and speak to the people staying there. We entered the metro tunnel and started walking.

I must say that was a strange walk. There you are, walking in semidarkness, behind whoever is in front of you, reacting to them telling you to watch your step. You can't really have a conversation because you're all strung out in a line. You drift along, listening to the vast underground silence.

Like any other normal person with odd desires, I've always wanted to walk between metro stations, of course. Yet I never thought that this was how it would go—a long crossing under a city that's fending off the enemy aboveground, holding out, not giving up, despite the shelling and attacks. From the depths, from underground, the city feels completely different: its breath, its energy, its silence, which can break out into a flurry of voices and cries. A city where you feel like you're where you should be, even when you're wandering between stations behind the mayor. :) Then we sang the national anthem at the station (I posted that video) and spoke to the kids and grown-ups. Then we brought them some things: food, warm clothes, sleeping bags, I think, and something else. Then the people staying there went outside into the city that had persevered. Then the metro started running again, and I hope it never stops.

I'm not trying to say that the war has become part of our memories or part of history. It hasn't become part of anything yet; it goes on, taking our lives, time, and energy. Nevertheless, imprints remain in our memories, they remain, like voices from the platform that comes after a black tunnel. After all, the city, protected by Ukrainian forces and marked by Ukrainian flags, remains.

June 13, 10:13 a.m.

I've thought about how certain places, symbols, and signs that helped us navigate the city before this full-scale war are now read or felt in a drastically different way. We are used to identifying the city based on certain landmarks: for some, it's the Derzhprom building or a university, for others it's Gorky Park or Barabashovo Market. Now the park, which has suddenly become the target of shelling (probably the most pointless shelling, considering they were targeting rollercoasters), will be seen quite differently, and Gorky should have been removed from the name a long time ago, along with Lenin.

Personally, my attitude toward Barabashovo has changed to a certain extent. And it's not my attitude toward the owners, of course—I don't know them—it's my attitude toward the people who work there. Back in early March, I remember going to see the boys who run stores there, and they loaded us up with everything they had left—everything that hadn't caught on fire—for us to give to the army: shoes, clothes, hygiene products, shovels, axes, staples, and other very useful things. These were the very same vendors whom people in town usually dismiss—*Oh, they're just trying to make a quick buck* is a common refrain. I'm not trying to make any generalizations. I'm just talking about what I saw, about the people I met by damaged pavilions, people I still talk to. In other words, this isn't an advertisement for the market. :)

I remember back in March, when things in the city itself were still pretty tough and chaotic, the very same vendors called and let me know that their colleague, who ran warehouses filled with military clothes, took everything he had left after the shelling to another warehouse, and we could head over there and pick up anything we needed for the cause, free of charge. That's when we were equipping our unit, Khartiya, and we needed clothes, uniforms, everything. So we headed straight to the warehouse.

It was in the middle of some shoreless Kharkiv industrial park, tucked between fences, tracks, hangars, and railroad crossings. It was quiet, empty, sunny, yet still cool. There was a vacant lot behind a large metal gate, and the warehouse stood in the middle of the lot. A young officer stood at the front door. He had received all these goods and begun handing them out to people who'd come from different units. An old German shepherd, confused and disoriented, was running between the cars. He had clearly been the one in charge before the war, running the show, keeping watch on everything. Now these young men in fatigues were managing everything. They didn't pay the dog any attention, which made him feel lonely and aggrieved. So he kept weaving between the cars, tripping people up, getting in the way, growing more anxious.

The officer was tired—said he hadn't slept in two days. He told us to grab what was there and not expect anything else. Because he was about to head out and get some sleep, and there was no telling when the warehouse would be open again (or whether it would ever be). We went inside. The vast space might have been full of equipment once, but all the good stuff had already been picked out and there was nothing left but scraps. Servicemen walked between heaps of clothes. It looked like an old bookstore with pensive bibliophiles roaming between the sprawling stacks. We started picking out T-shirts and shoes for a hundred people. The officer looked on with skepticism but wasn't stopping us or anything—take what'll fit, I don't need any of this.

Basically, now I know a little more about Barabashovo than I did before the war. :) Then we went back to the edge of town, leaving the industrial park behind.

The city stood: windy, torn, unapproachable, its church domes and blue and yellow flags blazing brilliantly. It was just getting started. And it still is . . .

June 13, 3:21 p.m.

We bought this wonderful Nissan for a unit we hold dear, Khartiya, and Oleh Abramychev drove it out to them. May it move quickly and stay out of the shop. This photo pretty much captures all the metamorphoses of the volunteer movement. :) I remember (yeah, yeah, I abuse that word, I know) taking tons of stuff to Kharkiv with Oleh during the first weeks of the full-scale war (mostly for the Freikorps)—everything from foodstuffs to bulletproof vests—and Misha Ozerov and his actors' volunteer hub would head out first thing in the morning and deliver humanitarian aid to basements and bomb shelters all over the city.

A lot has changed since then (although the actors are still volunteering and delivering supplies to elderly people who physically aren't in a position to stand in line at aid centers); now, first and foremost, aid is focused on servicemen.

Kharkiv fought off the first attack, but nobody can guarantee that our insane neighbors won't cause more problems in the future.

Basically, where there are Ukrainian forces there will be tranquillity. :) Thank you all for your support and assistance.

June 13, 9:25 p.m.

I've been reflecting on the fact that I carefully examine the likes and shares on my posts. It's not that things are that bad or anything. :) Some friends are in eastern or southern Ukraine, and sometimes you simply don't dare call them, like you're afraid of jinxing them or something. But seeing their hearts online puts you at ease—if someone near the frontlines has access to social media, they must be doing all right, more or less, and maybe you shouldn't disturb them. These are the simple yet crucial joys in a time of war.

Basically, I love you, my dear brothers and sisters. Rest up. Tomorrow, we'll wake up one day closer to our victory.

June 14, 2:48 p.m.

A word on urban planning. I remember an evening way back in '92 I spent with the brilliant Kharkiv artist Valer Bondar—may he rest in peace—a legend in the city and my spiritual mentor. We were riding a wintry tram from Zhuravlivka to the upper part of the city. Up Vesnina Street, actually.

It was cold and late, and Valer was bored. So he decided to put on an impromptu concert for the passengers. He pretended to be blind and began walking down the aisle, singing the melodies usually sung by orphans, howling with tremendous theatricality.

"Dear brothers and sisters! Any help is appreciated! Here's a kopek for you and a ruble for me. A kopek won't buy you a drink or a night on the town. I would have been a great opera singer, a second Sergei Lemeshev or Fyodor Chaliapin if that damn fascist bomb hadn't done a number on my head and my beloved wife Marusya hadn't left me!"

The passengers looked at Valer with hatred and fascination. These were working folks, weary from societal woes, who had no other mode of transportation.

What am I getting at? I like the fact that people have been talking about the future reconstruction of Kharkiv, about urban planning based on a completely different philosophy, about looking toward the future and abandoning the mistakes of the past. Looking toward the future is a good thing, even during a war. Especially during a war. I don't know if the Kharkiv of the future will have trams. I'm not an urban planner. I'm a poet. But for some reason, I think that trams fit into a European urban landscape more organically than a cardboard *marshrutka,* a van that follows a particular route, plastered with icons of Saint Nicholas.

Well, and I have some pretty good memories. The tram on Vesnina, for instance. Or on Pushkinska. Or in Kholodna Hora. In short, I'm all for urban planning that creates a particular atmosphere, has a human face, and is financially transparent.

This is a photo of the fire department—behind the tram—where Valer worked as a firefighter. Because what else should a brilliant artist do for work?

June 15, 7:35 a.m.

Maybe now I ought to start.
And no matter how much I told myself it wasn't
    time,
not to blindly mouth words
that aren't placed in my voice,
that aren't in books from a past life,
no matter how much I choked on the empty,
    wordless
air of this spring, the scorching, mute
air of the summer,
it turns out that language overpowers the fear of
    silence,
it should fill the breast pockets of life,
it should envelop the places people meet,
where they need to talk about themselves

so from then on,

they are recognized by voice.

Turns out that language rested like a March cold

in our lungs, weighing them down like clothes·
    on fugitives

swimming across a frozen riverbed.

It's also plausible that stripped of a voice we
    don't become

more honest with ourselves in our silence.

It's as if we've waived the right to sing in the
    choir,

afraid of ringing false, afraid of being offbeat.

And silence stands behind us like an unseeded
    field.

And muteness stands like wells packed with
    rocks.

Maybe this is it—our fear, our despair

account for the furious silence of bitter eyewit-
    nesses,

who saw everything they should speak to,

exposing murderers with song,

voicing their right.

The northern noise should be sown,

the mirage of morning melodies should be born.

There's an anxious feel to all this.

Since there's weight to all this.

June 15, 2022

June 16, 10:14 a.m.

I've loved Annunciation Market since I was a kid. Not for the selection or service, no. :) But for the atmosphere—to this day, you can still catch the spirit of an old city in Sloboda Ukraine, "a large industrial city, large, yet not trying to be grand," as Mykola Khvylovy put it. This place has certainly never been grand, but you can truly see that this city has by no means "forgotten its Sloboda birth, forgotten its Sloboda regiments," and that all the old ladies selling vegetables they grew in their own backyards, or all the folks from the towns or small cities outside Kharkiv, or the families from the upper part of town who come here to find a bargain are all Sloboda Ukraine or, at the very least, part of its fragmentary manifestations. Barabashovo Market doesn't have any of that—it has an international, multicultural feel to it. Well, thank God—I'm not trying to be critical. :) When the first vendors returned to Annunciation Market after the bombardment, we bought a bunch of stuff from them for our forces: chainsaws, axes, shovels, nails, construction staples, and tons of other things, all sold at a discount. I remember this one burly guy who had a huge pile of Soviet shovels (just where did he get them?) kept walking back and forth, and eventually he said, "I'll give them to you at prewar prices." :) Then he sat down right there on the curb for a while and sharpened the axes because he was clearly handy—literally, he did everything with his hands—and really wanted to help. It took him a while to count everything up—he wrote down everything in a notebook with a ballpoint pen, and we transferred the money to him because he didn't have a payment terminal. In short, he was clearly from Kharkiv's Podil neighborhood: real, simple, unpretentious, yet socially conscious and patriotic as hell in his heart.

Talking with guys like these, who are staying put, sitting at the market, selling their wares, and just going about their usual business kind of puts me at ease. We loaded up our car with everything we bought—which was an awful lot of metal—left the commotion of the market behind, crossed the bridge, and headed up toward the squares, theaters, and administrative buildings. Ukrainian flags fluttered above them, obviously. :)

June 16, 8:41 p.m.

We bought three compact GPS Garmin inReach® Mini 2 Flame Red satellite communicators for the 92nd Mechanized Brigade. For me, this is mystifying technology. But if the fighters say they need it, that's good enough for me.

We bought shoes for one unit so the boys could stand firmly and confidently on Kharkiv soil.

We gave our very own Khartiya several potbelly stoves to keep our boys warm in the field. And some backpacks, too. It's not much, but they'll come in handy. We ordered a bunch of other things, too. Now we wait.

In wartime, you aren't able to do what you're used to doing. To a large extent, this affects everyone, whether you're tilling the land or studying the humanities. Everyone has been swept up by the whirlwind of this war, torn away from where they've settled. But what I want most of all is for the fiendish force from the north to roll back over the border and for all well-intentioned people to regain the opportunity to do what matters to them. This is our land. We're used to looking after it. At the moment, it's hard to get our work done here—we have to support those who are wiping out the enemies of this land. In short, put your trust in the Armed Forces of Ukraine. :)

Rest up, dear brothers and sisters. Tomorrow, we'll wake up one day closer to our victory.

June 17, 8:21 a.m.

Good morning. :)

I'd like to say something, my friends—I keep thanking you for your support every day. And I'm being completely sincere, trust me. You can't even imagine how it feels when you don't have sufficient funds to purchase a car for our servicemen in the evening, and then by the next morning, you're able to come up with the full sum—from donations, both big and small—and you can purchase a car, drones, or other important things. I don't report on everything. Otherwise, my page would turn into an endless accounting book. For instance, people ask for a few thousand to repair a minivan or a military vehicle—they even send photos of the vehicles themselves. :) But they ask me not to post those photos, for obvious reasons. Others ask us to buy them a train ticket or to buy something here and give it to a relative who's fighting near Kharkiv. I don't write about everything here, but trust me, there really is a lot of work to do. Sometimes, though, I want to highlight certain things since they have symbolic significance, in addition to the purely financial side.

For instance, thanks to #artistsinshelter, a joint initiative between Translit and Kupido Literaturverlag, which was backed by the well-known European authors Nino Haratischwili, Yuri Andrukhovych, and Jan Wagner, we were able to raise 15,000 euros for Ukrainian artists and cultural figures in Kharkiv.

I'd like to thank all the donors, including Benefiz Puhlheim, Literaturhaus Hamburg, Julius Beltz Verlag, Berliner Ensemble, Schaubühne Berlin, and especially Nino Haratischwili, Mariana Sadovska, and Natalka Sniadanko, who, in addition to many others, were among the individual donors. It truly is important for us to feel solidarity with the artistic community and realize that people of art—both in Ukraine and beyond—are on the same wavelength and believe Ukraine will win.

We received the funds and will put them to good use. :) And in September, we'll try to hold a big literary festival in Kharkiv. :)

June 17, 4:39 p.m.

In my hometown, Starobilsk, the occupiers destroyed murals made by local youth. A drawing with my poem on it wasn't spared either—they just painted over it. By the way, the poem wasn't about Stepan Andriyovych Bandera or Symon Vasylyovych Petliura, or any other Ukrainian political figure from the past, for that matter. The poem was about a fish. But they painted over it anyway. The fish may have had traumatic associations with the Black Sea Fleet, which is currently sinking in Ukraine's territorial waters—I couldn't tell you.

Actually, the Russians, either consciously or subconsciously, are openly pursuing their primary goal, the real reason they're in our country. All their unconvincing nonsense about denazification and demilitarization is merely a way to cover up what they're really doing. De-Ukrainization—that's what they're doing. Burning library books, the Russian curriculum at schools, the dismantling of Ukrainian symbols—this, in addition to murdering, looting, and ruining cities, is a fully consistent politically motivated practice for them. They want to wipe us out. They want to wipe out everything in Ukraine that is a testament to Ukraine.

The thing is, though, they won't pull it off. And they'll have to answer for everything. I think those people who have somehow convinced themselves to collaborate with them, made up some reasons for themselves, feel this particularly well, very acutely.

We will return, even faster than they can imagine.
That's when we'll talk about poetry. :)

Written on the wall: (*First section, top left*): "Love, fish,
love"; (*bottom right*): "Albeit hopelessly, albeit" (*second
section, top left*): "Albeit without any hope at all"; (*bottom right*): "Rejoice, fish, rejoice / Serhiy Zhadan";
(*bottom center*): "Illustration by Khrystyna Lukaschuk /
@Black Sheep"

June 18, 8:33 p.m.

Year in and year out, the city in June was like a teen-ager spotting a brisk, flat river at the end of a long hike, sprinting toward the water, diving in headfirst, submerging fully, only to discover in the depths that the water hasn't warmed up all that much. Who's gonna let that stop them, though? Early June has repeatedly created an illusion of omnipresent sun and warmth so you don't really pay attention to the cloudy sky or the dismaying weather report because all you want is hot days, water, and greenery, all you want is to run out of springtime frosts and into summer like it's a river.

In June, Kharkiv used to be flooded with students, anxious, running all over at the end of the school year. Yet even their anxiety glistened with the anticipation of protracted summer idleness, idleness about to explode—they just had to pass that last exam. Classrooms emptied, and the air settled like water in a fish tank after the last desperate creature had leaped out.

This year, a completely different summer came to the city. Carefree passersby in parks and rowdy children among the trees elicit alarm, not ecstasy. Because evening will come, and the bombardments start in the evening. And these long summer evenings filled with listening intently to the slowly darkening sky—they tell you that a breezy, carefree attitude can't be artificial, you can't fake it. The war is so close; it'll always find a chance to remind you of that. It's not as though anyone has forgotten about it, though.

The greenery in June is still fresh and thick. Dust settles on the little streets outside town. We've got the whole summer ahead of us. We've got our whole lives ahead of us. People cling to this; people have something to love and lose.

Rest up, my friends. Tomorrow, we'll wake up one day closer to our victory.

June 19, 7:43 a.m.

I'm a real dummy when it comes to technology. I can't even use the calendar on my device—I do know the word "device," though. :) So I've always had a Word file named "Schedule for the Year," and year after year, I'd put everything I'd planned there. Sometimes I'd have up to three hundred events a year. At any rate, I would usually already know in January what I would be doing in August or September.

I recently realized that I haven't looked at that file for four months. And I'm not going to anymore. Because everything I had planned and written out has lost all meaning. Just like the old, pre-February sense of time has lost its meaning. Time has become compressed, like the ground under a strip of asphalt. At this point, everything is here and now, an arm's length away—you reach out and get everything you need. The very act of planning has lost all relevance because these days schedules depend entirely on the activities of the Armed Forces of Ukraine. This is a strange feeling, that time has been stripped of the weight it once had, that whole unutilized swaths of time that are no longer necessary have appeared. Time is frozen, in a way. It will pass at some point, but for now, this is how it feels here. Meanwhile, we're getting more and more summer. And the passage of time is mostly felt externally, visually—with the crowns of trees changing, with the color of the sky changing, with the ground becoming harder, stiffer.

Good morning, everyone.

June 19, 8:37 p.m.

We bought four drones for our servicemen. We'll hand them over tomorrow. Ukrainian troops have to be airborne and all-seeing. :)

Lately, I've heard a lot of stories told by friends I hadn't seen since late February. Each time, there are some marvelous—sad at times, quite humorous at other times—accounts of people accepting their new reality, stepping into it, establishing themselves in this new world, a world that changed forever at the end of this winter.

I suspect that these stories, these voices, these intersecting experiences and this hard, painfully ruptured coexistence await us all. The incisions that war makes in

the air are too deep and too painful, like they're wrenching apart roads we're used to walking down. Then we'll
have to patch up these roads—a bitter undertaking, but
one not without hope.

Rest up, my friends. Tomorrow, we'll wake up one day
closer to our victory.

June 20, 5:17 p.m.

We brought Khartiya some gifts: two drones, a generator, and a bag of underwear. :)

Each time, you see new faces in the field—more
and more new guys are coming in, the stream of people who want to defend the country has not ebbed. I'd
like to remind you that Khartiya is a volunteer unit; nobody is forcing anyone to join. It's very important for
these young people who are just being deployed to have
proper clothes, footwear, and equipment so they don't
go out into the field wearing sneakers. :) Meanwhile,
Kharkiv is all summer, greenery, and sun. There are a
lot of cars out, but not enough for there to be traffic jams
on Sumska or Pushkinska streets.

The city was struck by incoming fire in the afternoon. At the same time, moms walk down streets in the
city center with their children. Two realities reside here
somehow: a vast, translucent sky and smoke coming
from Saltivka.

Greenery ruptures the asphalt. Dust settles on the windows. Ukrainian flags flutter above the city.

June 21, 2:46 p.m.

We put on a concert for one of our units.

While we were singing, some Grad rockets landed nearby, and the power went out. The calm, confident commander just told us to wait a minute, though. :) Sure enough, the power came back on and we finished our song. As we were leaving, smoke rose into the sky nearby. :(The boys are cheerful and angry, too.

No drop in morale, no fatigue for them. They all want to crush the enemy. And that's what they're doing. :)

June 21, 7:29 p.m.

We bought a vehicle—didn't expect that. In Kharkiv. Sometimes you catch a break. :) We'd been promising one to the boys for a while, so we'll take it over to them tomorrow. We've been placing orders, receiving what we ordered, distributing, repacking, and preparing to deliver everything. It really is hot out there. :)

Lovers kiss with a sense of abandon on the benches in Shevchenko Garden. An organ grinder plays his own tune, something otherworldly, by the Shevchenko Theatre. Women sell flowers on the street; the people standing at bus stops are quiet and seemingly in no hurry.

The city center is calm, although the city has come under heavy bombardment. There are casualties. I've already written about one strike. Heavy smoke towered high. :(

The sky to the south is pure and translucent. Ukrainian flags flutter above the city.

June 22, 8:52 a.m.

There's been loud rumbling since yesterday evening. Several explosions were very intense—it felt like they were somewhere nearby, but picking anything out of the nighttime sky is hard and there's no way of knowing where one landed. Then a rain shower began, and its steady noise calmed things down. It's a brisk morning, filled with birdsong and the faint sound of car tires. We've loaded up two cars and we're headed into the field. Good morning, everyone. :)

June 22, 1:54 p.m.

We gave my friends from the unit two vehicles: a pretty, fashionable one and one we just got as a gift— which we really appreciate. :) The boys took them both.

They've been racing around in the pretty one, and they'll fix up the other one.

We also dropped off a ton of humanitarian aid, foodstuffs, and meds that the wonderful people from Vozko, a Ukrainian charity, had given us.

The town where the boys are stationed keeps getting hit. The Russians aren't sparing their expensive rockets, and they're destroying buildings and targeting civilians. :(

But our servicemen are holding their ground, fighting on, trying to help the locals. The war continues, everyone has stayed where they belong, and everyone is geared up to win. When you return to Kharkiv from the fields, it's like you're in a protected citadel. Kharkiv is all summer and tall grass. Ukrainian flags flutter above the city.

June 23, 6:14 p.m.

We gave our servicemen another drone. We're ordering another batch for specific units. Our troops are working. It's crucial that they have something to work with, so we keep helping out. And thank you for your support. We're moving toward our victory, step by step.

June 23, 9:09 p.m.

There's been constant movement in the sky since morning. The clouds drift, circumvent the outskirts of town. The sun pokes through, things heat up. But then the air fancifully fills with rainclouds.

Fresh footpaths have been forged along the tram tracks. The checkpoints we pass are somewhat calm and quiet, devoid of any anxious movement.

Cherry orchards on the edge of town blaze red.

The greenery outside the city is bright. It's as if the ground craves attention, calls more to itself, demands a little more love, which has been in such short supply this year.

It starts raining in the afternoon. The grass soaks it up, grows heavy and dark.

Radiance reappears in the sky in the early evening.

Clerks working at shops offer lazy and cheerful good-byes until the next morning, shout something humorous and upbeat at each other.

After the rain shower, the asphalt starts steaming, as if a warm riverbed flows deep below it.

Rest up, dear brothers and sisters. Tomorrow, we'll wake up one day closer to our victory.

June 24, 6:59 a.m.

Greetings to you all from blessed Sloboda Ukraine. Good morning, rise and shine. :)

June 24, 8:05 p.m.

Clouds have been hovering above the city and the edge of town all day. It feels like water is hiding in the grass like a living creature.

The stomach of the low-hanging, rainy sky grazes the tops of the trees. Wind rattles its dark, heavy branches.

Things are calm in the city, but friends talk about yesterday's strikes—the Russians destroyed an athletic complex near the city center.

A lively street market is open in Kholodna Hora; people sell what they've grown in their gardens.

The city center is empty. A woman determinedly sells flowers on Nauky Prospekt.

The late sun is dark red and smudged, like a stamp. It rolls along quickly, enveloped by clouds. It's evening, that's for sure. The night is coming. It's so quiet—just the way I want it to be.

Rest up, my friends. Tomorrow, we'll wake up one day closer to our victory.

The author remains in Kharkiv and continues to post daily on Facebook.

SERHIY ZHADAN was born in the Luhansk region of Ukraine and educated in Kharkiv, where he lives today. He is the most popular poet of the post-independence generation in Ukraine and the author of numerous books of poetry and prose, which have earned him national, continental, and international awards. His prose works include *Big Mac* (2003), *Depeche Mode* (2004), *Anarchy in the UKR* (2005), *Hymn of the Democratic Youth* (2006), *Voroshilovgrad* (2010), *Mesopotamia* (2014), and *The Orphanage* (2017), which won the 2022 European Bank for Reconstruction and Development Literature Prize. In 2022, Zhadan was awarded the Hannah Arendt Prize for Political Thought, as well as the Peace Prize of the German Book Trade for his "outstanding artistic work and his humanitarian stance with which he turns to the people suffering from war and helps them at the risk of his own life." He is the front man for the band Zhadan and the Dogs.

REILLY COSTIGAN-HUMES and ISAAC STACKHOUSE WHEELER are a team of literary translators who are best known for their translations of Serhiy Zhadan's prose, including *Voroshilovgrad, Mesopotamia,* and *The Orphanage.*